CARD
FORTUNE TELLING

CARD
FORTUNE TELLING

A LUCID TREATISE DEALING WITH ALL THE POPULAR AND MORE ABSTRUSE METHODS

BY

CHARLES PLATT

FULLY ILLUSTRATED

NEW ORLEANS : REBEL SATORI PRESS
MMXXI

Printed in United States of America & United Kingdom

Originally published by
W. Foulsham & Co., Ltd. London

CONTENTS

LIST OF ILLUSTRATIONS

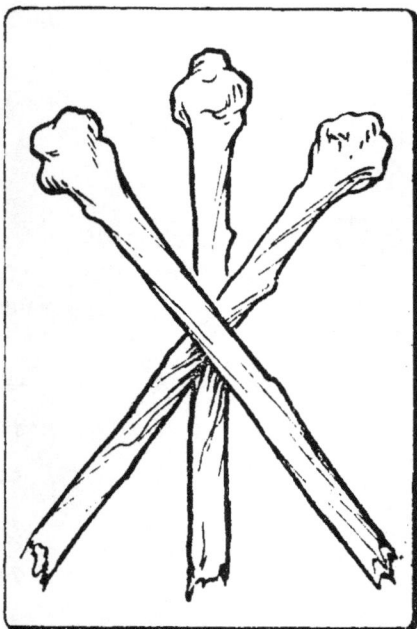

THREE of SCEPTRES [CLUBS]

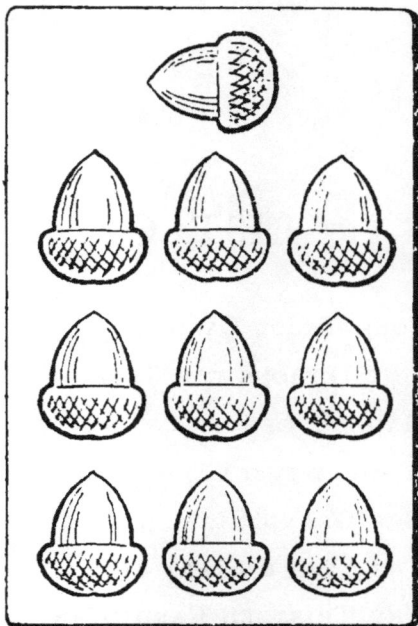

TEN of ACORNS [HEARTS]

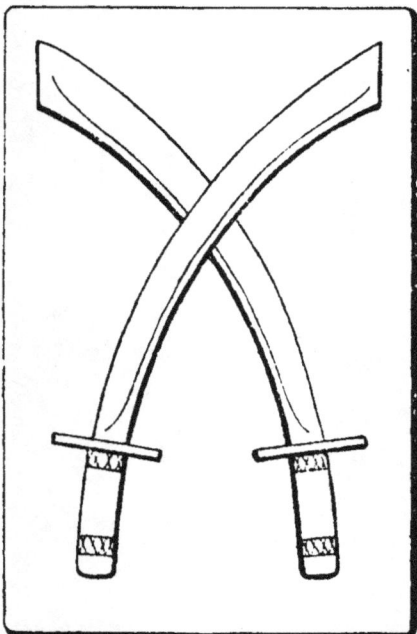

TWO of SWORDS [SPADES]

TEN of MONEY [DIAMONDS]

FOUR TAROT CARDS

CARD FORTUNE TELLING

CHAPTER I

A BRIEF HISTORY OF THE PACK OF CARDS

IT is a very popular belief that cards were invented in order to amuse King Charles VI of France, at a time when that monarch was mentally unstable. This legend, however, like so many pretty stories of the past, has no foundation in fact, as cards were known long before the mad monarch's days.

It is true that a court miniature painter, named Gringonneur, did paint or originate some cards which he introduced to the King, but cards were first used in the East in very ancient days, and it is a curious fact that the other great world-popular indoor game, Chess, also originated in the East, and is still played to-day by means of a pack of cards.

It also seems obvious that cards reached the West in the same way and by the same route as Chess, probably through the gipsies, that strange, unconquerable Eastern race of wanderers, whose actual origin still baffles our researches.

Naturally a race of people with no settled home or nationality would find much difficulty in moving their personal belongings from place to place, and would appreciate any amusement that could be reduced to the form of a pack of cards.

Chess was the great Eastern game, and is in many ways characteristic of a people to whom Time was of no importance. Cards may have been a game originally, but as known by the gipsies they were only used for the purposes of Divination, or Fortune Telling, and right up to the present day they still form the most popular and widespread means of testing the fortune.

Known as Tarocchi, or Tarots, the Divination cards numbered seventy-eight, and were without numbers—or pips, as we call them—which were introduced in Europe for the sake of simplicity, in the fourteenth century. Such packs are still in use in parts of the Continent, but the Western pack has gradually taken its place, both for the purpose of Divination and for playing games—in fact, it is usual to speak of a pack of " Playing cards," a distinction that is hardly necessary nowadays, as it is not easy to obtain a pack of Tarot cards, unless one knows where to go for them. The fact, however, that we still use this distinctive name, shows that at one time the two kinds were in use side by side.

If we compare a complete Tarot pack of cards with the modern Playing cards we shall find many interesting points of resemblance, and at the same time discover the reason for the changes made in the Western World.

There are twenty-one Tarot cards that are used solely for purposes of Divination, and the designs of these cards vary greatly and have probably never had any real significance. In addition to these, there is always a card known as the Fool—and as far as we know the card has always remained the same. For purposes of Divination it has no separate indication, but serves to intensify the meaning of the card next to it. Thus it becomes a very powerful and dominant card when one is foretelling the Future, as the indication supported by the Fool is certain to be active, and therefore must influence, or even suppress, all other indications.

Associated with a good card, the Fool is strong enough to carry you through much evil ; times may prove troublous, but you will pull clear before long. On the other hand, if the Fool is attached to a bad card, any signs of good fortune, shown by the other cards, will not be strong enough to save you from the threatened trouble, though they may modify it to some extent.

It is a curious fact that in certain card games we still find this all-powerful Jester, who has the happy power of over-trumping the Ace of Trumps, whatever the suit may be. Apart from this, our modern pack of Playing cards has entirely abandoned the twenty-two special Divination cards of the Tarocchi, though these cards were and still are used for games as well as for Divination purposes in those countries where the Tarot pack is still in regular use.

In addition to these twenty-two cards, the Tarot pack contains fifty-six cards, divided into four suits, just as our modern packs are divided. But the superior Western mind has destroyed all the original clever significance of the Tarot, and has substituted the senseless jangle of Diamond, Heart, Club and Spade—meaningless, senseless, nonsense !

In the Tarot, the four suits are represented by other emblems :—we have the Vase, which represents the Priestly caste of the East ; the Sword, which indicates the Warrior caste ; the Piece of Money, which clearly shows the Merchant caste ; and finally the Baton or Club gives us the Yeoman or Tiller of the soil.

Here then we have four suits of cards, each one representing a distinct class of people, and in the quartette are covered all classes of the people—for in the early

Eastern days the Priestly caste were the rulers, and chose the King or nominal ruler. They were quite capable of " removing " him peacefully if he did not follow their bidding. So our four suits give us the Rulers, the Fighters, the Merchants, and the Farmers.

We will now compare these four ancient Tarot suits

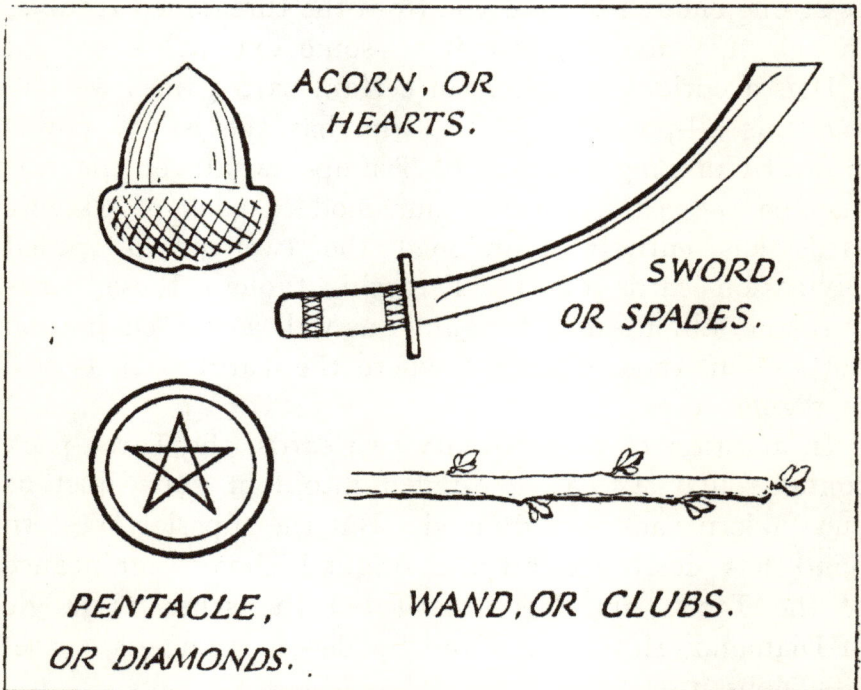

ACORN, OR HEARTS.

SWORD, OR SPADES.

PENTACLE, OR DIAMONDS.

WAND, OR CLUBS.

SUIT DESIGNS FOR TAROT CARDS

with our modern Western nonsense—Hearts, Clubs, Diamonds and Spades !

The Vase or Cup of the Tarocchi cards has become the Heart of the modern pack ; this is an easy change, as the bowl remains, while the stem has been thickened to complete the heart shape design. Although this suit originally represented Religion or the Priestly caste, it was never considered what may be called a " lucky " suit, in the modern sense of the word. Curiously enough this has always been the suit we now call Clubs, which originally represented the Tiller of the Soil.

Obviously there is a sound philosophy in this arrangement, for the mass of the people were indirectly taught that good fortune would follow their own personal exertions, and that they should not blindly rely upon the favour of the high gods.

This suit has been variously represented in the past ; the Baton is shown sometimes as a branch with sprouting leaves ; it seems probable that our modern Club is derived from the lucky Trefoil, a very old and widespread superstition. It may represent the " business " end of a spade, with the shortened handle turning downwards. Anyhow the Club or Trefoil suit is the lucky one for Divination purposes.

It is easy to see how the Piece of Money, originally a crudely squared piece of metal, changed into the Diamond, with its modern association with wealth; and it is also quite clear that the Spade represents the handle and blade of a Sword, typical of the fighting caste.

It is important that we should clearly understand these changes before we consult the cards as to our future, because the modern suit names are merely nonsensical, whereas the original Tarot suits assist us to follow the reasoned meanings given to the various cards.

Here, then, in the old Tarot pack of fifty-six cards, as also in the modern Playing pack of fifty-two cards, we have four typical suits. It is difficult to account for the alteration in number, unless it was done out of respect for the " Thirteen " superstition, that being the fateful number in all Divination. Yet the original fourteen cards to the suit was not altered for Divination purposes, but purely for games ! This appears so contradictory that one is almost forced to the belief that there must be some other explanation.

It is important that we should notice that the Tarot suits contained ten numbered cards, as in the modern pack, and also four principal cards, now known as Court cards, which originally consisted of King, Queen, Knight, and Jack, four natural grades of rank, if we look upon the Jack as the " common people."

For some unknown reason, the Knight was omitted, but the idea of the four Court cards was actually retained, and the simple " One " of the suit was promoted over the head of the King. It seems to me probable that this was an attempt to retain the Fool, which really forms part of the more important section of the Tarot pack, which was *not* used as a full pack of seventy-eight cards, but a sort of twin pack, with a Major, or Great Arcana of twenty-two cards, and a Minor, or Lesser Arcana of fifty-six.

Having reduced the pack to fifty-six cards, the loss of the Fool was quickly realised, and the *lowest* card of each suit was then made into a sort of limited or local Fool, with the power of the original Fool, of trumping the King, though only of his own suit. This superstitious introduction of what amounted to a fifth Court card caused the throwing out of the Knight, and the universal adoption of our curious modern pack, which consists of four Court cards and ten commoners, yet only contains thirteen cards !

This explanation of the reduction of the pack to fifty-two cards appears to be confirmed by the later appearance of the Piquet pack, popular in France and on the Continent—here the pack is reduced to thirty-two cards, four Court cards and four commoners in each suit. As the " One " card had been promoted to the proud position of Fool or Ace, it was natural—though absurdly illogical—to continue the reduction from that end of the pack. Thus we have the very ridiculous pack containing Seven, Eight, Nine, Ten, and the four Court cards.

If the Piquet pack had been derived from the original Tarot pack of fifty-six cards, it would undoubtedly have contained One, Two, Three, Four, Jack, Knight, Queen and King.

It is a very curious fact that there should be four suits in a pack of cards, although as already shown these balance nicely with the four Estates : Priests or Rulers, Warriors or Fighting Men, Merchants or Artisans, and the Tillers of the Soil or common people. An early Eastern form of the game of Chess was a four-players variation, each alternate player partnering his *vis-à-vis*, just the same as in modern Bridge or Whist. The two partners in this form of Chess used pieces of a similar colour—two using red pieces, the other pair using white or *black!* Then from the East, dating from about the same period, we have the four suits of the Tarocchi cards, again two red and two black.

All this points clearly to a common Eastern origin for Chess and Cards, and the probability seems to be that card playing or Divination has been derived from Chess. It is worth noting that there is an obscure form of Chess in which the pieces are all off the board at first, as are the cards in the hands of a player ; they are placed on the board or table one at a time, as the player's turn comes round, and they are not active till they are thus displayed—just as in card games.

In the early years of the fifteenth century, the art of engraving was perfected, and printed coloured cards came into use in place of the old hand-painted packs. About the middle of that century, the present suit symbols were first used, on French cards of the reign of Charles VII. Thirty years later, we find many references to " Chess and Cards," showing the close popular connection between the two games.

It is a curious and fascinating point in this study of the history of cards, that the German invention of engraving was directed to the production of packs of cards— not books ! The printing of the Bible in 1455 followed shortly after the production of the first packs of engraved cards. The earliest suit values, apart from the original Tarot suits, were Hearts, Leaves (Trefoil, now Clubs), Acorns (Diamonds), and Bells (Swords or Spades).

So popular were the comparatively cheap engraved packs of cards that every artist turned his attention to them, and for some years the suits were represented in scores of ways, before settling down to the modern universal and somewhat senseless series of Hearts, Diamonds, Clubs, and Spades. Thus there were figures of men and women, birds, beasts, fishes, flowers—some cards were square or oblong, some circular. In all these early engraved packs, as in the ancient Tarot examples, every card was a full design—the simple pips of to-day date from the beginning of the sixteenth century, and are probably the result of a number of indecent—or at any rate indelicate—designs being produced.

It is important to remember that there was no actual Queen on the genuine ancient Tarocchi cards, nor was there a Queen in their game of Chess—in both cases this change was made in the dandified atmosphere of Western European Court circles. The original design was a Vizier or Prime Minister—naturally in the Far East, and especially in those early days, women were conspicuous by their modest absence from public view. But quite apart from that, both Chess and Cards are really fighting games, and were used by warriors when not professionally engaged.

Thus we have the King, his Vizier or General, his Knights or Warriors, the Jack or Knave, thought by some to represent the King's sons, though more obviously the well-to-do people, and the commoners. It is worth noting that an old Eastern form of Chess was played on a board of ten squares each way, thus absolutely agreeing with the ten commoner cards of our Tarot and Playing packs. It seems probable that a ten-piece game, with superior pieces or cards, was the original source of our modern Chess, with its eight common and eight superior pieces, as well as of our modern Playing cards, with the original ten commoner cards, but only three distinct superior cards, together with the double position of the Ace, which represents One in some cases and the Fool in others.

In the following chapters, we shall describe all the best recognised methods used for Divination by cards. It does not follow that we believe in what is technically known as Cartomancy, nor in the rigidity and certainty of our so-called Fate. In fact, a rigid belief in Fatalism, so prevalent in the East, at once destroys all our personal responsibility for our actions, and destroys all incentive, all ambition, all striving for better things. It is solely due to this lack of striving that the East has remained almost stationary in progress for so many centuries, while the less superstitious West has gone rapidly ahead.

The easy doctrine of Fatalism has much to answer for !

Still our lives are full of remarkable coincidences, many of them impossible of explanation. It would be absurd to dispute the fact that we are all greatly and permanently influenced by our surroundings and by each other. The general principle of Heredity is well understood, but no one knows how far-reaching its remorseless grip may go. It is impossible for any thinking, reasonable person to deny that the Present—or the Past—does and must influence the Future—to what extent this may go is still a mystery.

The essential feature behind Cartomancy is exactly the same as in several other forms of Divination—the person whose future is to be read *must* in some way influence matters. Some Diviners use a Crystal that has been held in the hands of the questioner, who thus personally affects the Crystal, and, so it is claimed, causes visions to appear therein. Other Diviners ask for some personal article, closely associated with the person whose future is in question. Obviously this method is not quite so safe, as it is practically impossible to use any article that is solely personal to one individual. A glove or handkerchief is often used, but it seems perfectly clear that either of these must carry many other influences besides those of the owner. A lock of hair seems best, but even then there may be the influence of one's hairdresser or one's maid—especially a lady's-maid, who would handle her mistress's locks every day in the ordinary course of her duties.

To a great extent this question of " mixed " influences must also affect the Crystal, apart from the close intimate touch of the Diviner if he or she holds it in the hands. For this reason a black velvet pad is often used for the support of the Crystal after the questioner has handled it.

But it is obvious that this precaution cannot be fully effective, as each questioner in turn must handle the Crystal, and thus affect it, though to what extent is not known. The most accurate result I have ever come across, and it was startling in its exact truth, was made with a Virgin Crystal, that had never before been used for Divination. On the other hand, the most hopelessly ridiculous was made at a big gathering of people interested in occult subjects. Here the " atmosphere " should have been sympathetic in the extreme, yet the unfortunate Crystal-gazer admitted that she had been all at sea the whole afternoon, and could not explain it. It seems only too obvious that the Crystal itself had become confused with the rapid and continuous change of " influences," as questioner followed questioner, every few minutes.

It is claimed that Cartomancy avoids all such troubles, because the shuffling of the cards by the questioner is the essential starting point, not a mere personal touch or usage of some article. There seems to be much sound sense in this argument, and if that is accepted, then Cartomancy justifies its claims both as a simple and as a reliable means of Divination.

Cartomancy has an additional advantage—and fascination—in the fact that the cards can be dealt and arranged in so many different manners, and it is quite usual for two or more of these to produce somewhat similar results. I have frequently found that one particular point is emphasised in this way, though the additional minor points may, and should, vary.

I claim that these minor points should be expected to vary, because the personal influence of the questioner must also vary from moment to moment. We find this in everyday life, and it appears to be an essential of our very existence. For a whole day, a full week, even for a month or more, our main and principal thought may concern one particular person or matter, yet every moment of that time our minor thoughts will concern themselves with scores of different ideas.

It would therefore be hopelessly ridiculous to expect the cards to repeat any one set of details concerning the questioner's future ; indeed, one cannot reasonably expect the repetition of even one dominant point, unless the questioner has sufficient will power to keep his or her thoughts steadily upon the one point.

If you use the Cards, or the Crystal, to oblige a friend who is idly curious, you may deal in twenty different ways and never get two that agree. What else can you expect !

It is therefore advisable to make sure that your sitter is really in earnest, and then persuade him or her to concentrate their thoughts upon one principal dominant idea—let it be what it will. Then you may reasonably expect to get good results.

Let me give one earnest word of warning—never offer to pretend to " foretell the Future " ; that is impossible. As far as we know, there is *no* definite, fixed, or rigid Future for any one of us—all you can do is to point out how the subject is drifting ; how he or she is likely to be placed or affected ; whether a certain thing, desirable or unpleasant, is likely to come about—never that it *will* come about.

Free will is the key-note of all Dame Nature's efforts, and every one of us is master of his own Destiny, within the limitations of his own personality. Bear that clearly in mind when you read the cards. Never state that a thing *will* happen, but that it appears probable in the present course of affairs. For instance, if an illness is indicated, it may in many cases be avoided altogether, or greatly modified in its effects, if reasonable care and precaution are taken. It is just the same with people and affairs—we need not drift their way, if we choose to struggle against them.

The Future is in each person's own hands, but the fall of the cards, if correctly interpreted, may serve as a warning against possible dangers that lie ahead of us, or alternatively they may serve as a stimulus and cause us to put forth still greater efforts to secure some desirable result.

Before describing the various methods of Card Divination, I should like to point out that it is not necessary to memorise the various meanings of the cards. The simplest plan is to use a special pack, and mark the meanings and combinations on the face of each card. In this way you avoid all tedious references and quickly learn how to read from any particular fall of the cards.

It is not considered possible to work for your own information with any degree of accuracy, but that need not prevent your regular practice with the cards. Shuffle and cut as if you were a stranger to yourself, ask any reasonable question that occurs to you, and in that way endeavour to gather from the fall of the cards what answer you would give a stranger under similar circumstances. Practice will soon make you proficient, and will open your eyes to the wonderful combinations that are possible under Cartomancy.

Begin with an ordinary modern pack of Playing cards, but go on to the full Tarocchi Divination. You need not be extravagant over the purchase of a genuine Tarot pack, but can easily cut twenty-six cards of the ordinary size, upon which you can write the necessary descriptions. For the Tarot Divination cards, you need only number your blanks from one to twenty-one ; then you need a Fool, and finally the four Knights, one for each suit. In this way you can obtain a cheap and very interesting pack of Tarot Divination cards, with which you can entertain, and possibly help your friends.

Should you have any artistic powers, or happen to know any gifted friend, these extra cards can be ornamented and coloured to your own fancy, provided you insert the necessary numbers. In fact, it would not be a difficult task to design and paint a full pack of Tarot cards for your own use—in which case a visit to the British Museum or the Guildhall would give you some useful ideas upon which to base your designs.

In the modern printed packs, there is much needless monotony, but in a genuine Tarot pack, or in a modern hand-painted pack, no two cards would be alike. For the Heart suit, you would introduce one Cup in an upper corner for the Ace, and so on ; otherwise you can let your fancy rove how and where it will. One suit could represent Flowers, another Animals, a third a series of Women's Costumes of various ages, a fourth Birds—you can vary them to any extent, though each suit should show a similarity of thought for all the cards.

NOTE.—A pack of seventy-eight Tarot Cards, with guide, can be obtained from the publishers of this book, for 8/6 post free.

CHAPTER II

METHODS OF GREAT DIVINERS

MADAME LENORMAND

THE pack consists of fifty-two cards—four suits of thirteen each. Each suit consists of the Ace, King, Queen, Jack, Ten, Nine, Eight, Seven, Six, Five, Four, Three, and Two—or alternatively of King, Queen, Jack, Ten, Nine, Eight, Seven, Six, Five, Four, Three, Two, One.

It has been observed that this fourfold division of the pack corresponds to similar divisions of Time, which are thus set out :—

1. Diamonds.	2. Clubs.	3. Hearts.	4. Spades.
1. Youth	2. Manhood	3. Maturity	4. Age
1. Spring	2. Summer	3. Autumn	4. Winter
1. Morning	2. Noon	3. Evening	4. Night

The fifty-two cards correspond to the fifty-two weeks in the year, i.e. the four Suits to the four Seasons of thirteen weeks, such as shown above. Of these, Spring includes March, April, and May; Summer includes June, July, and August; Autumn includes September, October, and November; and Winter completes the circle of the year with the months of December, January, and February.

This only applies to the modern pack, as the real Tarocchi packs contain fourteen cards to each suit.

Each card, taken by itself, and in connection with that preceding and following it, i.e. one, two, and three cards at a time, will give seven possible combinations. Now, $7 \times 52 = 364$, which, added to the pack or unit, gives 365, the number of days in the year. So, then, it will be seen that the pack of fifty-two cards corresponds at all points with the natural divisions of time.

The Ace of each suit rules the first week of the corresponding Season, and is followed by the King, Queen, Jack, Ten, etc., declining till the lowest card, the Two, is reached.

The value or signification of the four suits is briefly as follows :—

Diamonds denote Life in general, and for this reason are largely dominated by the accompanying cards.

Clubs denote Power, whether arising from affluence, fame, position, or inherent capacity.

Hearts denote Love and its inflexions, such as friendship, sympathy, attachment, together with peace, tranquillity, and the concomitants of love.

Spades denote Loss, privation of any sort, things in their ultimate issues. The suit is capable of many inflexions, however, and, like the Diamonds, shines only by the reflected light of accompanying cards. Hence a run of Spades has no light in it at all, and is sinister and ominous in the extreme.

Every consultant has a corresponding card in the pack which is allotted to him or her as a significator. With men it is a King, with women a Queen, and the suit is controlled by the colouring or complexion of the consultant.

Diamonds signify very light people ; blue eyes or grey,

and flaxen or red hair. They also denote persons grey or white-headed with age

Hearts denote fair people, darker than the Diamond type, with blue or grey eyes and brown hair.

Clubs denote brown-eyed people, with brown hair; the average brunette type.

Spades denote very dark people, almost black or raven-coloured.

N.B.—A Club in the case of a widow or widower becomes a Spade. A Heart in similar cases becomes a Diamond.

Boys and girls are denoted by the Jacks of the Suits, according to their colouring; and the sex is shown by the King or Queen nearest or touching them.

The Jacks in general denote attendants, servitors, servants, attachés, followers, etc., thus :—

Jack of Diamonds, a carrier, postman, messenger.

Jack of Clubs, an agent, business man, clerk.

Jack of Hearts (Cupid), a lover, follower, friend.

Jack of Spades, doctor, physician, or professional man, down to the undertaker.

The Court Cards (Kings, Queens, and Jacks), and all even numbers, are qualified as good or bad, according to the attendant cards, i.e. those falling in juxtaposition.

All odd numbers, including the One, are good when the right way up, and bad when reversed.

With one or two exceptions, the systems of card-telling now in use are those handed down to us by the Bohemians, and employ only a part of the ordinary pack.

That in most repute used only thirty-two of the cards, rejecting the Two, Three, Four, Five, and Six of each suit.

The following meanings attach to the thirty-two cards employed :—

DIAMONDS

Right way up		Reversed
Ring, letter, banknote	Ace	Letter to pay bill, &c.
Fair or grey-haired man, widower	King	Flattering, treacherous
Widowed Queen of Heart, fair friend	Queen	Jealous coquette
Military, public servant	Jack	Spiteful man
Money, town, success	Ten	Journey, anxiety
Sharp instruments, news	Nine	Accidents, danger
Short journey by road or rail	Eight	Spite, worry
Young person, child, pet	Seven	Small gain

CLUBS

Right way up		Reversed
Success, good - luck, papers	Ace	Delayed letter, writs, bad news
Faithful, generous man	King	In trouble, worried
Devoted friend, respected	Queen	In perplexity
Virtuous lover	Jack	In ill-luck
Money received, luck, journey	Ten	Estrangement, voyage
Happiness, legacy, a will	Nine	Obstacles
Money, love of a dark man	Eight	Agreements, contracts, etc.
Victory, success	Seven	Perilous undertaking, financial trouble

HEARTS

Right way up		*Reversed*
House, love-letter	Ace	Upset, change of house
Good-hearted, loving	King	Capricious, uncertain
Affectionate, fair woman	Queen	Revengeful, jealous
Friend, lover	Jack	Disappointment, delay in love
Happiness, fortune	Ten	Birth, change
The wish, success	Nine	Affection, troubled
Love, success, invitation, clothes	Eight	Trouble, jealousy
Favours, flirtation	Seven	Jealousy in love

SPADES

Right way up		*Reversed*
High building, love, profession	Ace	Vexation, trouble, death
Widower, lawyer	King	Enemy, avaricious man
Widow, faithful friend	Queen	Plotting and treacherous woman
Professional man, doctor	Jack	Traitor, deceitful man
Voyage, water, great distance	Ten	Sickness, mourning
Failure, remote hope	Nine	Death, disappointment, delay
Illness, night	Eight	Quarrel, deceit, seduction
Change, removal	Seven	Accident, loss, theft

These are the simple meanings of the cards. Their complex meanings when in combination with other cards can only be learned from experience. It is here that the intuitive faculty has its full play.

Take, however, a simple illustration as a guide to the general method. The King of Clubs falling between the Nine of Spades and Ace of Spades (reversed) would indicate that the consultant, if a Club man, is in immediate danger of death or of very severe illness bringing him near to death. If, however, an Ace of Diamonds and a Ten of Hearts were on either side of the King of Clubs, he would be on the eve of marriage and in a very happy condition of mind.

Several Court cards coming together show assemblies, gatherings of people, and festivities, public functions, etc. ; with the Ace of Spades, in a church, theatre, or other high building ; with the Ace of Hearts, at the house of the consultant, and so on.

The Kings all coming together show business ; the Queens thus placed show talk and scandal ; the Jacks, workmen about the house, agents, and servants, danger of trickery ; and if evil cards add their testimony, it may be detectives or bailiffs, creditors, and other unpleasant visitors.

The Aces falling together denote new surroundings, with success or failure according to the cards that follow them ; but the Aces always show a change of life when falling together.

N.B.—If the consultant be married, the King or Queen of the same suit must always be taken as the husband or wife.

POSITION

Much importance attaches to the position in which any card falls in relation to the significator.

Above the significator denotes success, achievement, the wish gained.

Below, denotes that which is past, completed, obtained, the condition in which the consultant now is.

Right of the significator shows aspiration, desire, hope, effort, that to which the consultant is approaching.

Left of the significator shows things that obstruct the path, difficulties to be surmounted, that which delays success or opposes the desire of the consultant.

These are called Direct Positions. The Oblique Positions are as follows :—

To the Right, above, shows things that help forward the gain of the wish, and conduce to success.

To the Right, below, shows things accomplished in the direction of the wish of the consultant.

To the Left, above, shows what obstacles will arise out of the past to prevent the wish.

To the Left, below, shows things that have already arisen in the past.

If the Nine of Spades, the "disappointment" card, falls touching the significator, it is a sign of the wish not being accomplished. If the Nine of Hearts touches, it will bring the wish. If both of these cards touch the significator, the wish will be delayed. If they touch one another, the wish will be changed. Among other things the Nine of Spades shows a wet day.

Observe that Clubs and Hearts generally denote success, while Spades denote failure. Diamonds are uncertain and depend on the cards attending them—that is, preceding, following, or touching. The Ten of Hearts is always a corrective to bad cards when falling with them.

A point to which attention must be directed here is that a reversed card has its meaning modified. In some packs it is fairly easy, by noting the difference in the top margins, to detect a reversed card. But generally speaking, now that card printing is so regular, it is better to ensure the detection by marking the cards at one end by a little dot.

Usually only thirty-two cards are used for fortune telling—the Twos, Threes, Fours, Fives, and Sixes being thrown out. In one method that will be detailed thirty-six cards are used—the four Twos are added. The Tarot pack consists of seventy-eight cards, but in some of the delineations only a part of these are used.

Generally the meanings of the cards remain fairly constant for all the methods. Thus a good omened card is always such—but the particular or specific meaning of it is altered somewhat by the method of using it. For example, the Ten of Spades by one method means " losses," and if reversed, " tears " ; in another, " grief," and if reversed, " passing trouble." The Seven of Spades may mean " hope," and if reversed, " friendship " ; or it may be " resolve," and if reversed, " difficulty in love affairs."

These meanings, or values, of the cards should be well studied and committed to memory, so that when any particular card appears, a key to its interpretation is at once presented to the mind of the reader. The word key is used advisedly, because these terms or values are not to be taken as the absolute determination of the cards, but rather as a guide to the specific values in relation.

In this connection it is as well to note the meanings of combinations. It is easy to imagine that Hearts generally are associated with love and marriage. This suit is also closely related to domestic matters, and to the social amenities of life. Diamonds are generally associated with financial considerations, and though, as has already been suggested, they are modified by other cards coming close to them, they are usually emblems of a favourable character.

Clubs are almost always good. Successful enterprises,

contentment in home life, and prosperity in worldly undertakings are indicated by Clubs. Spades are the unfortunate suit. If connected with love it is usually of an unreciprocated nature. Sickness, losses, and deaths and monetary embarrassments are all indicated by Spades.

If there is a run of a particular suit it will be seen that Clubs will be an omen of the brightest character, while a similar run of Spades will indicate the worst possible phases of fortune. A run of Hearts will foretell successes in love, of Diamonds in money. Combinations of Court cards are important. Amongst others the following may be noted :—

When the Aces come together they denote new surroundings. How this will affect the future fortune depends upon the influence of the cards that follow them.

Sepharial suggests that the Aces coming together portend always a change of life. Foli thinks they imply danger and financial loss. But this is lessened if they are reversed ; three Aces, temporary trouble. It should be remembered that the modern Ace, when not used as the One, represents the old Fool, which had the power of upsetting or changing everything. Bear this in mind when reading the cards.

Kings coming together denote business, or as another authority has it, " honours, preferment, good appointments." If reversed, of less value, but arriving earlier. Three Kings are a good omen unless reversed. Four Queens imply talk and scandal, or a social gathering, spoilt if the cards be reversed. Three Queens denote friendly visits, but if reversed possible danger to the consultant. When the Jacks come together, workmen or agents about the house, or roistering and noisy conviviality. Three betoken annoyances from friends. If reversed the evil is not so considerable.

Four Tens and four Nines stand respectively for good fortune and surprises. Three Tens are very bad, but three Nines good. Four Eights, a mixed omen of success and failure. Three Eights, new family ties. Four Sevens, trouble is imminent; three, ill-health, loss of friends.

Nine of Diamonds and the Eight of Hearts together is regarded as a sure indication of a journey. Ten of Clubs, followed by an Ace, betokens a large sum of money. A sequence of Ace, King, Queen, and Jack of one colour foretell Marriage, so also do the Ten of Hearts and Ace of Diamonds. When the Nine and King of Hearts appear together, they form a good combination for lovers.

Before proceeding to lay out the cards in any of the methods detailed in the following pages, the card-teller must take the pack in hand and proceed to shuffle them. This is for the purpose of getting rid of the influence of any other person who may have been handling the cards recently. The pack is then handed to the consultant, who is required to shuffle it very thoroughly.

The attitude of mind in which this shuffling should be done depends upon the purpose for which it is effected. If the general fortune, past, present, and future, is required, then let the consultant maintain a passive mind, neither anxious nor intent, but wishing only to know the truth, and to accept, without cavil or protest, anything the diviner may predict from the cards.

If, however, a definite "wish" is required, then let the mind of the consultant be intent upon its nature and the source of its gratification. Let this mental attitude be steadily maintained while the "shuffle" is being made.

In regard to this process of shuffling the cards, it will be observed that it is of the most vital importance, since the order in which the cards are subsequently laid out cannot be altered when once the shuffle is completed. Some of our readers may think that nothing reliable can be drawn from a proceeding which is so obviously a matter of chance. But let such for a moment consider the propriety of using such a word as chance.

The cards having been duly shuffled, the consultant must cut the pack into three parts at hazard, turning the cards thus cut face upwards. In almost every case it will be seen that the three cards thus displayed will correspond to the nature of the consultant's thoughts, the wish, or what is uppermost in his mind, or nearest him in event.

If a lady is consulting and she cuts the Ace of Diamonds, Jack of Hearts, and Ten of Hearts, without doubt her present lover will make her a gift of a ring. If she were to cut her own significator (say the Queen of Clubs) together with the King of Clubs and the Eight of Hearts, it shows a lover in the shape of a dark man.

If instead of the Eight of Hearts, the Eight of Spades were cut, she would, if married, be in danger of a quarrel with her husband, and her thoughts of him would not be kind. If unmarried, she would be about to quarrel with a dark man, denoted by the King of Clubs. In this manner the various combinations will denote what is " in the wind " as regards the consultant. The cards are taken up by the Diviner in the original order, the backs being uppermost. They are then laid out according to any of the following methods. The cards must be shuffled and cut before each and every " lay," the cut being duly noted by the Diviner.

Two of the best known exponents of Card Divination were the famous French consultants, Madame Lenormand and Monsieur Etteila, as he was known professionally. We shall begin with these proved methods, as they are practised and recognised all over the world.

c

MADAME LENORMAND'S NINES

This method employs thirty-six cards, viz., the Ace, King, Queen, Jack, Ten, Nine, Eight, Seven, and Two of each suit. The cards are laid out in rows of nine each from left to right.

The place on which each card falls will determine in what manner it will affect the consultant. Each place has a definite name, and rules over that element in the life designated by its name.

The thirty-six positions are named as follows :—

1	2	3	4
Project	Satisfaction	Success	Hope
5	6	7	8
Risk	Desire	Injustice	Ingratitude
9	10	11	12
Acquaintance	Loss	Hurt	Estate
13	14	15	16
Joy	Love	Luck	Marriage
17	18	19	20
Pain	Happiness	Inheritance	Treachery
21	22	23	24
Rival	Gifts	Loving	Elevation
25	26	27	28
Benefit	Enterprise	Change	Death
29	30	31	32
Reward	Disgrace	Good fortune	Wealth
33	34	35	36
Indifference	Favour	Ambition	Sickness

We strongly advise the reader to copy this plan in a size large enough to take full-sized cards, either on linen or card. (See Fig. on page 48.)

The cards touching the significator of the consultant must be regarded, i.e. those that are above, below, right, and left of it, and those that touch it obliquely to the right and left, above and below. These nine cards (including the significator), taken in relation to the positions they occupy, will determine the condition of the consultant, his hopes, success, obstacles, and dangers.

The other cards are then interpreted one by one, according to the positions they occupy together with their general signification.

In this latter respect the Two of Diamonds signifies the confidant of the consultant ; it also serves for widows and widowers, or the lover of the consultant, or anyone inquired about.

The Two of Hearts denotes the consultant, or the person for whom the cards are drawn.

The Two of Clubs denotes a parent or an adviser of the consultant.

The Two of Spades denotes anyone or anything represented by the position it occupies, having no definite meaning of its own.

The cards may be drawn twice—the first time to learn what events lie in the near future, the second time to know those more distant. In each case the operation is identical, remembering always to shuffle and cut before each deal.

THE THIRTY-SIX POSITIONS

1. *Project.*

Hearts.—Success in undertakings, when a Heart card falls in this position. The cards accompanying, viz., in positions 2, 10, 36, will show the particulars of success.

Clubs.—A faithful friend will work to bring about success for you.

Diamonds.—Difficulties caused by jealousy or spite. Note accompanying cards.

Spades.—Treachery and serious delay.

2. *Satisfaction.*

Hearts.—Your wish will be accomplished. Many favours await you.

Clubs.—Fidelity will surmount all difficulties and give you joy.

Diamonds.—You have difficulties to overcome by reason of much jealousy.

Spades.—Treachery will diminish your hopes of happiness.

3. *Success.*

Hearts.—Happy and favourable prospects surround you.

Clubs.—By means of friends you will gain your desire and have success in your projects.

Diamonds.—Many difficulties owing to jealousy and distrust. Nevertheless you will succeed according to your merits.

Spades.—Deceit and treachery. There is little hope of success herein.

4. *Hope.*

Hearts.—You will gain your wish.

Clubs.—You have good chances of gaining your wish, but you will have to work hard towards it.

Diamonds.—Hopes lightly founded or entirely vain will not meet with fulfilment.

Spades.—A foolish hope inspires you. Be prepared to see it destroyed root and branch.

5. *Risk.*

Hearts.—You will enhance your fortunes by means of

unexpected gain. Whatever you have at stake will yield you a good result.

Clubs.—You will be benefited and put in the way of securing a better condition than you now are in. You will succeed fairly well.

Diamonds.—Expect unlooked-for things. If you ask about money at stake you will get it. In other respects your surroundings are uncertain. Look at the cards touching this number. If Hearts or Clubs, good ; if Diamonds, money ; if Spades, expect loss by fire, water, or other unlooked-for event.

Spades.—Very bad risks. Unfortunate speculations, thefts, losses, and even bankruptcy.

6. *Desire.*

Hearts.—You will gain the object of your most ardent desire. Your wishes will be fulfilled.

Clubs.—With effort and by the assistance of others you will accomplish your wish.

Diamonds.—Others are interested as well as you. There will be contention and some risk of failure.

Spades.—Alter your wish. " All hope abandon ye who enter here." Your wish cannot be granted.

7. *Injustice.*

Hearts.—An injustice has been done you, but you will have full reparation and your rights will be recognised.

Clubs.—Employ an intermediate. You have every hope that your merits will be regarded.

Diamonds.—Make overtures in the shape of presents and gifts. Nothing stands in your way except a feeling of annoyance.

Spades.—Forget your wrongs, and do not augment them by affording fresh opportunity for injustice to be done to you.

8. *Ingratitude.*

Hearts.—You will be pleased to receive proof that those who have been ungrateful are anxious to make amends.

Clubs.—Your friends will make redress of all slights and ingratitude you have suffered.

Diamonds.—Do not be annoyed, jealousy alone is at the root of the ingratitude you have received.

Spades.—Do to others as you would have them do to you. Expect disappointment and treachery, but see that you do not offend in this respect yourself.

9. *Acquaintance.*

Hearts.—Your associations will be profitable to you. Certain friendships will be of great advantage to you.

Clubs.—You have the best of friends. See that you do not neglect them.

Diamonds.—Beware of being a cause of jealousy and strife among your associates.

Spades.—Exercise the greatest caution in selecting your friends, but do not be surprised if you are betrayed. You may be of use to others, but will get little from your associates.

10. *Loss.*

Hearts.—Be prepared for the loss of benefactors and those of good heart towards you.

Clubs.—Your affairs will receive a rude shock by the loss of a friend.

Diamonds.—Guard your possessions and interests, for there is danger of severe losses at hand.

Spades.—Deceit and treachery surround you in business. Grief and trouble through losses await you. Beware of false investments, frauds, and thefts.

11. *Hurt.*

Hearts.—Your affections will receive a hurt which will give you much pain.

Clubs.—Friendships will give you sorrow and trouble. Expect the loss of a friend.

Diamonds.—Your interests and business affairs will cause trouble. Spite is directed against you.

Spades.—Much sorrow is at hand. Be prepared for grief, losses, and treachery.

12. *Estate.*

Hearts.—You are going forward towards success from day to day.

Clubs.—By means of work and good friends you will progress to your satisfaction and acquire wealth.

Diamonds.—With some worry and a good deal of opposition you will have success.

Spades.—Your estate is falling away. Redouble you. efforts and your care, and be watchful of your interests for some time to come.

13. *Joy.*

Hearts.—You will have cause for joy in the direction where your affections are placed.

Clubs.—Happiness will come to you through your friends and your efforts.

Diamonds.—You will be gladdened by overcoming an obstacle in face of opposition and jealousy.

Spades.—You will be glad to have been of use to others. Faithful service to a superior will bring its reward.

14. *Love.*

Hearts.—You will have success and happiness in your love

Clubs.—You have a faithful lover who will advantage you in many ways.

Diamonds.—Jealousy, the green-eyed monster, besets the path of uncertain devotion.

Spades.—Your affections will be blighted ; but do not despair, you will conquer at last by patience and fidelity.

15. *Luck.*

Hearts.—You will have success in life, and prosperity is now coming to you through legitimate means.

Clubs.—By your own mental and moral efforts, as well as the help of good friends, you will have more than enough to live honestly.

Diamonds.—There is danger of your fortunes being affected seriously through jealousy and rivalry.

Spades.—Hate and deceitful dealing will destroy your chances of immediate success.

16. *Marriage.*

Hearts.—You will marry well. One whom you love will reciprocate your affection.

Clubs.—Your friends will be the means of bringing about your marriage. It will be a well-assorted match.

Diamonds.—Trouble, worry, and vexation follow on marriage. If you are in quest of a dowry rather than a wife you will get it. The consequences you must bear with resignation.

Spades.—Treachery and malice are the fruits of marriage in your case. Beware how you choose a partner. The Nine of Spades here means divorce, the Eight means separation.

17. *Pain.*

Hearts.—Your troubles will soon pass away. Live in hope.

Clubs.—Effect a reconciliation with your friends as soon as possible.

Diamonds.—You are troubled because of sharp words and angry feelings. Dismiss them and live in peace.

Spades.—You are the victim of deceit and treachery. Bide your time and do not take active measures yet.

18. *Happiness.*

Hearts.—Your affections are well placed and reciprocated. Nothing hinders your happiness.

Clubs.—With prudence and attention you will touch the springs of happiness.

Diamonds.—You seize pleasure with too desperate a hand. You run great risks and are liable to excite anger and jealousy.

Spades.—Your pleasures will be of short duration. Be careful they are not the cause of your undoing.

19. *Inheritance.*

Hearts.—You have every reason to expect a considerable inheritance.

Clubs.—You may expect a legacy from a friend.

Diamonds.—You will engage in strife and legal proceedings which will cost you more than you gain by legacy.

Spades.—If you have any right to an inheritance there is great danger of your losing it by means of deceit on the part of others. Look well ahead, and provide for contingencies.

20. *Treachery.*

Hearts.—Rest assured that the evil directed against you by false friends and traitors will fall on them alone.

Clubs.—You will have time to thank your friends for a timely deliverance from plots directed against your welfare.

Diamonds.—Time will efface the effects of treacherous plots and spiteful actions. But you will be very much upset by discovering the danger you are in.

Spades.—Scandal, loss of friends, and deceitful dealing are to be expected.

21. *Rivals.*

Hearts.—You overcome all rivalry. The day is yours. Make the most of it.

Clubs.—Your own merits and the good offices of friends will secure you a victory over your rivals.

Diamonds.—Through some spite and intrigue you may hope for a decision in your favour. The omens are fickle.

Spades.—You cannot hope for success in this direction. Your rivals will secure all the favours you expect.

22. *Gifts.*

Hearts.—You will have gifts far exceeding your expectations.

Clubs.—Gifts will be made to you for your own sake. Favours from friends.

Diamonds.—Be careful of being drawn away from the path of honour by gifts of money and other inducements.

Spades.—Beware of any gifts made to you. Treachery and deceit are hidden under smiles and overtures of friendship.

23. *Loving.*

Hearts.—You will be satisfied in the love bestowed on you. You have the affections of a person of good character.

Clubs.—You have one of good birth in whom to repose your affections. You will receive benefits from your friends and confidants.

Diamonds.—Be careful. Your lover is susceptible to jealous feelings. Beware of strife among your friends.

Spades.—You will have cause to regret having placed your affections in a certain quarter. The person is vindictive and deceitful. Your friends are hypocritical and false to a degree.

24. *Elevation.*

Hearts.—You will rise far above your expectations, and become the object of regard and honour among worthy people.

Clubs.—By the fulfilment of your duty you will obtain elevation and competent fortune. Do not neglect your friends.

Diamonds.—Rivalry and contention will for a long time defer your advancement.

Spades.—Treachery and malice will obstruct your upward path. You are advised to serve and not to strive for mastery.

25. *Benefit.*

Hearts.—You will receive all the reward you merit, and many benefits from your superiors.

Clubs.—You will gain benefits through your friends, to whom you will owe a great deal.

Diamonds.—You will only gain part of the benefits you merit owing to contentions and jealousy.

Spades.—The benefits you merit will go to another because of misrepresentation and falsehood.

26. *Enterprise.*

Hearts.—Your undertakings will meet with success, and you will make your mark.

Clubs.—Your ventures will be lucrative, and your friends will be of much use to you in your undertakings.

Diamonds.—There is too much competition and rivalry in your field of enterprise. You are liable to be outdone.

Spades.—Many of your enterprises will turn to your disadvantage. You will need to look after your affairs with great care and caution.

27. *Change.*

Hearts.—You will have a happy and advantageous change in your fortunes. Luck attends you.

Clubs.—You will have to thank a friend for a change in your condition which will be of much good to you.

Diamonds.—Be careful lest you are thrown out of the frying-pan into the fire. Avoid strife.

Spades.—You are in great danger of losing your present position. You have secret enemies to contend against.

28. *Death.*

Hearts.—Through a death you will gain something you do not expect.

Clubs.—A friend will benefit you by a legacy.

Diamonds.—You will soon hear of the death of an enemy.

Spades.—Your worst enemy is near to death. Your worst days are coming to an end.

29. *Reward.*

Hearts.—You will gain the reward of your labours, and your fidelity will be requited with abundant esteem.

Clubs.—You will receive the reward of your work. By means of your friends you will gain all for which you have striven.

Diamonds.—Your recompense will be diminished or retarded by jealousy.

Spades.—You are in danger of losing by deceit that which is promised or expected.

30. *Disgrace.*

Hearts.—You will soon forget whatever little disgrace you may incur. It will turn to your advantage.

Clubs.—A friend is in danger of disgrace. You will resent it. It will pass away.

Diamonds.—You will suffer from calumny and spite. Be careful your name is not brought into just reproach.

Spades.—You have misplaced your confidence, and in consequence will suffer loss of honour. You will be betrayed.

31. *Good Fortune.*

Hearts.—An unexpected stroke of luck will render your condition a very agreeable one.

Clubs.—You will receive a considerable increase in your fortune by the aid of friends and supporters.

Diamonds.—Jealousy and the ambition of false friends will be to your advantage.

Spades.—In case of pressing need you will receive the assistance of friends. You will be in great danger, even to the life, but you will be providentially protected.

32. *Wealth.*

Hearts.—You will make a brilliant fortune, quite equal to your highest ambitions.

Clubs.—Your work and intelligence, aided by the services of friends, will secure you a fortune of some extent.

Diamonds.—Persons of an avaricious and jealous nature in whom you have placed confidence will make their fortunes at your expense, or will profit greatly from your own fortune.

Spades.—Your energies and talents are doomed to enrich others only. Be therefore discreet in the use of your energies, and try to preserve your rights.

33. *Indifference.*

Hearts.—You will be indifferent to the future of others, and will thereby lose some of the happiness of life.

Clubs.—Your indifference in the choice of friends will often cause you grave anxieties.

Diamonds.—Others will gather the fruits you neglect through your indifference to your own interests.

Spades.—Neglect of duties and general apathy will cause the loss of money, honour, friends, and health.

34. *Favour.*

Hearts.—You will have the favour of wealthy persons,

who will advance your interests very much. You are fortunate in gaining affection and esteem.

Clubs.—By your sagacity and fidelity you will gain many friends and will receive many favours from them.

Diamonds.—You will have difficulty in obtaining any very substantial favours. You have many rivals.

Spades.—You had better depend upon your own labours and the fruits of your work, for little or no preferment will accrue to you.

35. *Ambition*.

Hearts.—Pursue your ambitions with steadfastness and you will reap your reward.

Clubs.—You will accomplish your ambitions by means of your friends, who will take an interest in your schemes and projects.

Diamonds.—The jealousy of relatives and friends will cause many of your ambitions to fall short of attainment.

Spades.—You will suffer a serious disappointment in your chief ambition through the treachery and malice of false friends and secret enemies.

36. *Sickness*.

Hearts.—Your illness will be of short duration. It will be nothing.

Clubs.—You have nothing to fear. Your illness will not be dangerous.

Diamonds.—Sharp but short illness will prostrate you for a while.

Spades.—You will not suffer alone. Your enemies are also afflicted with sickness. But beware of a long trial and have patience.

Note.—Hearts show good fortune wherever they fall, and promise success. Clubs show assistance from friends and well-directed personal effort. Diamonds are fickel and show spite, envy, and jealousy.   Spades indicate failure, treachery, malice, and lack of initiative.

When good cards surround the number under consideration, it gives an augury of the best results ; but if Spades or Diamonds fall thereon, and are surrounded by good cards, it promises obstacles and delay.   When Spades fall thereon, and are surrounded by evil cards, such as Jacks, Spades, and Diamonds, it portends failure in that particular indicated by the number.

The following numbers deserve special comment :—

No. 5 equally shows all risk by lottery, cards, or other games, racing, things burnt or flooded, and speculations of all sorts.

No. 6 denotes all and every object of desire, whether money, love, legacy, or anything not as yet attained and not depending on one's own efforts, as do the ambitions, No. 35.

No. 7 shows equally the result of all lawsuits, adjudications, the recompense of superiors, etc.

No. 9 includes all associations, such as marriage, partnership, friends, and business engagements.

No. 16. If the consultant be married or under age, then the interpretation is capable of modification.

No. 21. This includes all kinds of rival interests, whether in marriage, love, business, or competition.

Project   Satisfaction   Success   Hope   Risk   Desire   Injustice   Ingratitude   Acquaintance

Loss   Hurt   Estate   Joy   Love   Luck   Marriage   Ruin   Happiness

Inheritance   Treachery   Rival   Gifts   Elevation   Loving   Benefit   Enterprise   Change

Death   Reward   Disgrace   Good Fortune   Wealth   Indifference   Favour   Ambition   Sickness

MADAME LENORMAND'S METHOD

CHAPTER III

IN the illustration (p. 48) of an actual " falling " of the cards, it will be noticed first of all that the Two of Hearts, representing the consultant, is reversed—this fact must be borne in mind while we interpret the cards.

Of the eight surrounding cards, three represent people, two of these being men ; House number Twenty-one, where the Two of Hearts rests, signifies Rivalry of all sorts, not only in love, but in business. It is good that a Heart should fall here, but the reversed position at once suggests delay or interference, which is also confirmed elsewhere.

Let us now consider the Suits of the eight cards ; we find that we have three Hearts, including the Fool, who has the power of changing everything unexpectedly. As this card falls in House Thirty-one, showing Good Fortune, we again see that all will come right, but in some un-expected fashion. There are also two Clubs, which show the influence of friends ; two Diamonds, and only one Spade. This is a very fortunate series as far as suits go ! The Eight of Spades is not a very bad one, and signifies ill-health in all probability, especially as the personal card is the only reversed card in the series.

The combination of the Ace of Diamonds in House Twenty-two (Gifts) with the Ten of Clubs, on either side of the personal card, suggests the unexpected receipt of money. We must also note the presence of the Queen of Clubs and the Seven of Hearts, which strongly suggest favours through a woman, and in all probability the Jack of Hearts, in House Eleven, represents a rival in the affections of the woman in question.

This brief sketch will give an idea of " how it is done," but the Diviner must cultivate the power by shuffling and arranging the cards, time after time, until he or she can recognise the combinations with some ease.

We must not, however, overlook the other indicating cards—for instance the Two of Diamonds represents the confidant of the enquirer, and in the present case, this card falls on House Eighteen—which signifies Happiness. In the diagram it appears to be a long way from the Two of Hearts, but in reality it is only two places away from the vital group of nine cards, with the Queen of Hearts between—this is a good card, and signifies a generous or affectionate woman, thus intensifying and confirming the previous reading.

The Two of Clubs is too far away to affect your Divination, though it falls in the Marriage House, and is next the Eight of Diamonds—a journey, probably to the home of the woman who is so vitally concerned in this matter.

Madame Lenormand's method of Card Divination is an excellent one and is much favoured. It has the great merit of simplicity, and the use of the four Twos as indicators avoids disturbance of the Court card values.

It is necessary to point out that the full nine cards can only be obtained when the Two of Hearts falls in one of the centre rows. Obviously if it falls in the top row, you can only use six cards. In this case I myself assume that the bottom row has been transplanted above the series, and in this way I secure the full nine cards. For instance, if the Two of Hearts had fallen in House Four, instead of the Queen of Diamonds, then the three extra cards would be the King of Diamonds, Ace of Hearts, and Eight of Hearts.

In the same way, if the Two of Hearts had fallen in House Thirty-five, instead of the Two of Spades, then you would add the Nine of Diamonds, Nine of Hearts, and Jack of Spades. Obviously this also applies to the sides, when the indicator card, the Two of Hearts, falls in Houses One, Ten, Nineteen, Twenty-eight, on the left, or Nine, Eighteen, Twenty-seven, Thirty-six, on the right.

This point should be carefully studied, because the four extreme corners will necessitate a double readjustment. Thus if the indicator card falls in House Nine, instead of the Jack of Spades, the nine vital cards would be the Nine of Hearts, Eight of Diamonds, and Two of Diamonds, already touching the Two of Hearts, together with the King of Hearts, Ace of Spades, Two of Spades, Seven of Diamonds, and Ten of Diamonds. This makes a very complicated mental readjustment until you get used to it.

There is another great advantage in Madame Lenormand's method—you can easily get a definite answer to a simple straightforward question. Let us suppose that some such question has been asked in the present case, and the cards, after shuffling, have fallen as in the diagram. You merely have to study the suit values of the eight cards surrounding the Two of Hearts, after adjusting them mentally should the indicator card fall on an outer row.

In the present case we find three Hearts, two Clubs, two Diamonds, and only one Spade—a very fortunate arrangement—so you can safely promise the enquirer a fortunate result to his question, whatever it may be.

Hearts are the most fortunate, and signify our own

exertions or efforts ; Clubs also are favourable, but signify friends and their efforts on our behalf—Diamonds are neutral in fortune and signify delay, while Spades are bad. In this case the proportion is five favourable cards against two neutral and only one bad card.

Again you will notice that there are two Heart Court cards, including the Ace or Fool, which dominates everything else and is very powerful ; one Club, two Diamonds, but no Spade. So in every way your reply can be satisfactory. You must remember that in addition to the direct Yes or No, the fall of the cards may indicate partial success only; a failure of our own efforts, but success through our friends ; partial success, and so on, dependent upon the fall of the suits and the proportion of Court cards included in the eight surrounding cards.

CHAPTER IV

ALTHOUGH Madame Lenormand's method is wide-spread and popular, there are many other fascinating ways for dealing the cards. To make a change, we now give a method which can be followed with the full pack.

Of the different suits, Clubs stand generally for happiness and rarely are of bad omen. Next come Hearts, which are not so deep in their significance and show joy, liberality, good temper. Diamonds denote delay, quarrels, annoyances; while Spades are the fateful suit, and signify grief, misfortune, illness, death. It is important to pick up the cards quite haphazard, as those which are reversed in the pack have quite a different significance. Such cards as the Ace, Ten, Nine, Eight, etc., of Diamonds should have a small pencil mark to show the top.

Shuffle the pack well, cut the cards three times, and lay them out in rows of nine cards each. Select a King or Queen to represent the person who is consulting you—Hearts representing blonde types; Diamonds the ordinary fair people; Clubs the brunettes, and Spades the very dark ones. Some well-known users of the cards allow their consultant to choose any King or Queen to represent themselves—this, of course, must be done before the cards are touched. If preferred, the pack can be cut, and the exposed card would indicate the suit to be used.

Having dealt your cards in the above way, look for the

type card and count nine every way, reckoning the type card as number one. The cards thus indicated will be the prophetic ones. In the case of a married woman, the King of the same suit of which she is the Queen would represent her husband, and should be counted from in a similar way, as the marriage partner's influence is naturally of great importance. In the case of a married man, the reverse applies, the Queen of his own suit representing his wife.

The Jack of the type suit shows the thoughts of the person, and they also should be counted from.

The meaning to be attached to the various prophetic cards is as follows :—

The Club Suit.

Ace.—Peace of mind, happiness, a success card.

King.—The influence in your life of a dark man, upright, faithful and affectionate.

Queen.—A brunette, gentle and pleasing.

Jack.—The thought of the King for the questioner. In the case of any Court card, you should count nine in every direction from it for the prophetic cards for your guidance.

Ten.—Unexpected good.

Nine.—Disobedience to the wishes of friends.

Eight.—A warning against speculation.

Seven.—Good fortune and happiness if you are careful in your dealings with someone of the opposite sex.

Six.—Business success.

Five.—A prudent marriage.

Four.—Be careful of changes in your plans or mode of life.

Three.—Indicates a second marriage.

Two.—A disappointment, but not a serious one, unless other prophetic cards are bad.

Take notice of all the prophetic cards before making any conclusions from them.

The Heart Suit.

Ace.—This indicates your home, and if Spade cards touch it quarrelling is foretold.   If other Hearts are next to it they foretell friendships and true affection.   If Diamonds, money and distant friends—and if Clubs, feasting and merry making.

King.—A fair man, good-natured but rash.

Queen.—A fair woman.

Jack.—This covers the thoughts of the dearest person of the one who consults the cards.

Ten.—Refers to children. It also softens the bad tidings of the cards near it and increases the good.

Nine.—Money and position.   Also, where the cards are consulted about one single question or wish, the Nine of Hearts is the key card upon which all depends.

Eight.—Pleasure, companions.

Seven.—A false friend.

Six.—A generous person.

Five.—Troubles caused by jealousy.

Four.—A person near you, not easily convinced.

Three.—Sorrow caused by your own indiscretion.

Two.—Success, but it will need care.

The Diamond Suit.

Ace.—A letter.   You must look at the surrounding cards to judge the result.

King and Queen.—A fair man or woman.

Jack.—Thoughts as before.

Ten.—Money.

Nine.—Travel.

Eight.—A late marriage.

Seven.—Unpleasant rumours, scandal.

Six.—Early marriage and possible widowhood.
Five.—Unexpected news.
Four.—Trouble through friends, a secret betrayed.
Three.—Quarrels and legal troubles.
Two.—An engagement, but against the wishes of friends.

The Spade Suit.

Ace.—Great Misfortune. Death when the card is reversed.
King, Queen and Jack.—Dark people and their thoughts.
Ten.—Grief and trouble.
Nine.—Sickness and misfortune, a most unlucky card.
Eight.—A warning to be careful.
Seven.—Loss of a friend, much trouble.
Six.—Money through hard work.
Five.—A bad temper that causes trouble.
Four.—Sickness.
Three.—A journey.
Two.—A removal.

Be careful to notice if two or more cards of the same value come together.
Two Aces.—Trickery.
Three Aces.—Good news.
Four Aces.—Danger and failure.
Two Kings.—A business partnership or the joining with a friend in some enterprise.
Three Kings.—Important business, generally successful.
Four Kings.—Rewards, dignities, public honours.
Two Queens.—A meeting with a friend.
Three Queens.—Visits.
Four Queens.—An entertainment of some sort.
Two Jacks.—Evil intentions.
Three Jacks.—False friends.
Four Jacks.—A noisy party, drinking.

Two Tens.—Change of profession or business.

Three Tens.—Indiscreet conduct.

Four Tens.—Great and certain success.

Two Nines.—A small gain.

Three Nines.—Good health and fortune.

Four Nines.—A great surprise.

Two Eights.—A brief love dream.

Three Eights.—Contemplation of marriage.

Four Eights.—A short journey.

Two Sevens.—Indiscretion.

Three Sevens.—Sickness and failure of strength.

Four Sevens.—Trouble from servants or employees.

Should any of these cards be reversed, it greatly lessens the strength of the combination—thus, it would increase an evil influence, but would lessen or destroy a good one, and merely show that such a happy possibility had been lost.

We stated that the cards carrying most meaning were the ninth cards in every direction, and we will make this quite clear by an illustration. Let us suppose that the fifty-two cards are arranged in rows of nine as follows :—

7C	7S	KS	AD	AH	JC	4H	8H	JS
2D	3D	2H	6H	KD	5C	2C	5S	3H
5H	6D	4C	QC	5D	3S	KH	4D	10S
9S	QS	8D	6C	AS	QD	KC	JH	6S
9H	10D	8C	7D	AC	9C	9D	JD	10H
10C	8S	QH	7H	4S	3C	2S		

A FIFTY-TWO CARD METHOD

If the King of Hearts represents the person who consults the cards, we shall find this key card in the third row ; it is indicated as KH. We can now count nine to the right, reckoning the key card as one. Our third card, however, finishes the row, so we have four routes open to us : (1) to turn upwards and keep to the outer cards, in which case the ninth card would be the Ace of Hearts which we know to represent the home, and as no Spade card adjoins it, all should go well. (2) We can turn downwards and keep to the outer cards, in which case we reach the Seven of Hearts, indicating a false friend, and touching this card are a fair woman, a warning against speculation, unpleasant rumours, a success card (Ace of Clubs), an illness—the presence of the Ace of Clubs just saving us from a very ugly series of disasters. (3) We can turn upwards, and continue along the second row, in which case we reach the Six of Hearts, a generous person, which is surrounded by a brunette woman, a warning of care in changing plans, a note of success if care is taken, a dark man, a letter, a fair man, and unexpected news— other people are far too much mixed up in the life and plans of the enquirer and great care is necessary. (4) We can turn downwards and proceed along the fourth row and thus reach the Six of Clubs, business success, which is surrounded by unpleasant rumours, warning against speculation, a late marriage, a warning against change of plans, a brunette woman, unexpected news, a fatality, and a success card (Ace of Clubs)—a most unpleasant mixture, just saved from disaster by the Ace of Clubs !

The key card itself, the King of Hearts, is surrounded by a dark man, a fair woman, a journey, a prudent marriage, a slight disappointment, temper, trouble with friends, the thoughts of someone—so it seems reasonable to assume that a marriage, rather late in life, probably with a woman as fair as or fairer than himself (the Queens of Hearts, Clubs, and Diamonds are all among the cards to which we have referred, but the only Jack, for thoughts, is that of Hearts), and a fresh home, made after a journey, will see our subject through his troubles, but that bad temper and quarrelling will certainly be one result.

It is a recognised rule in " telling the cards " (as it is called) that they should only be consulted again after an interval of nine days on behalf of any one person. But it is quite a frequent practice to mix the pack thoroughly, re-shuffle and cut and deal as before for a second and a third time at one sitting, carefully noting all the cards that come into view each time, and thus averaging the result of the three attempts.

It would, however, be wiser to vary the counting of the nines instead—thus, for a second attempt, you could count to the left instead of to the right ; or you could count upwards or downwards from the King of Hearts. All four ways would lead to a different series of cards, and thus a greater degree of accuracy would certainly be attained.

Let us examine the results very briefly—thus, by counting to the right, as already worked out in detail, the cards that we come in contact with are :—Hearts—Ace, Two, Six, Seven, Jack, Queen. Clubs - Ace, Two, Four, Five, Six, Eight, Jack, Queen, King. Diamonds— Ace, Four, Five, Seven, Eight, Queen, King. Spades— Ace, Three, Four, Five, King.

The following simple table shows at a glance the results of all four methods :—

Heart Suit.

Right Count :   2, 6, 7, J, Q, A.
Left Count :   2, 5, 9.
Up Count :   2, 3, 4, 5, 6, 8, J.
Down Count :   3, 7, 9, J, Q.

Club Suit.
 Right Count : 2, 4, 5, 6, 8, J, Q, K, A.
 Left Count : 4, 7, 8, 10.
 Up Count : 2, 4, 5, 7, J.
 Down Count : 3, 8, 9, 10, J, A.

Diamond Suit.
 Right Count : 4, 5, 7, 8, Q, K, A.
 Left Count : 2, 3, 6, 8, 10.
 Up Count : 2, 3, 4, 6, A.
 Down Count : 4, 7, 9, 10, J, Q.

Spade Suit.
 Right Count : 3, 4, 5, K, A.
 Left Count : 7, 8, 9, Q, K.
 Up Count : 5, 6, 7, 10, K.
 Down Count : 2, 4, 5, 6, 8, 9, 10, Q.

The cards surrounding the Heart King are included in the right count in the above Table. It will be noticed that by following this full method of using the cards that *four* key cards are reached twice over—they obviously are the most important. They are the Three of Diamonds, showing quarrels and legal troubles ; the Nine of Hearts, showing money and position ; the Seven of Hearts representing a false friend ; and the Ten of Spades indicating grief and trouble. This confirms our previous reading that the enquirer will have much trouble and difficulty, but will eventually win his way through.

In the above Table it will also be noticed that certain cards appear once only—they are of little importance to the enquirer. Those that appear twice are seldom worth considering, but the really important are those that appear three or four times—the latter being very rare, of course. There are seven cards, however, that appear three times in the present experiment and we quote them in full.

Heart Suit.

Two.—Success, but it will need care.

Jack.—Thoughts—this card appears next the Heart King.

Club Suit.

Four.—Be careful of changes in plans.

Eight.—A warning against speculation.

Diamond Suit.

Four.—Trouble through friends—this card also appears next the Heart King.

Spade Suit.

Five.—Temper and quarrelling—this also touches the enquirer's personal card.

King.—Obviously the dangerous friend.

In this way also we get a startling confirmation of our prediction, which is taken from actual experience and has proved correct.

The method of Card Divination that we have just described is known as the English—not because it originated over here, but to distinguish it from the many continental methods where only thirty-two cards are used. We will now give some English methods based on the Piquet pack, of thirty-two cards, as used on the Continent.

The thirty-two cards are those used for an ordinary Piquet game—you throw out all the lower value cards from Two to Six, both inclusive. The cards, therefore, run from the Seven to the Ace. The meanings of the cards necessarily vary from those of the English method, and we therefore give them in full. The Kings, Queens, and Jacks, represent people and thoughts as in the English method.

The Club Suit.

Ace.—Money, good news, happiness. If reversed, it is of short duration.

Ten.—Fortune, social success, luxury. If reversed, a sea voyage.

Nine.—Unexpected gain. If reversed, a trifling present.

Eight.—A dark person's affections. If reversed, unhappiness will result from it.

Seven.—A small sum of money. If reversed, money troubles.

The Heart Suit.

Ace.—A letter, pleasant news. If reversed, a visit from a friend.

Ten.—Happiness and success. If reversed, a disappointment.

Nine.—This is the wish card, and if it turns up near the enquirer's own Court card, the wish will be granted. If reversed, some passing anxiety in connection with the wish.

Eight.—A fair person's affections. If reversed, indifference in place of love.

Seven.—Pleasant thoughts, tranquillity. If reversed, weariness.

The Diamond Suit.

Ace.—A letter. If reversed, bad news.

Ten.—Journey or change of abode. If reversed, it will not be fortunate.

Nine.—Annoyance, delay. If reversed, a quarrel.

Eight.—Love making. If reversed, unsuccessful.

Seven.—Mockery, unpleasant news. If reversed, scandal.

The Spade Suit.

Ace.—Pleasure of an emotional nature. If reversed, grief, news of a death.

Ten.—Tears, sometimes a prison. If reversed, a brief affliction.

Nine.—Tidings of a death or failure. If reversed, loss of a near relation.

Eight.—Warning of illness. If reversed, a marriage broken off.

Seven.—Slight annoyances. If reversed, folly on the enquirer's part.

If two or more cards of a value come together, they should be judged by the Table given for that purpose under the English method, as it is universally employed. A number of small Spade cards together show a certain financial loss. The Queen of Spades indicates the death of husband or wife, unless it is the type card of the enquirer, who would have to be a very dark woman.

Speaking generally, the Heart cards govern the affairs of the home, and therefore the love affairs of the enquirer. Diamonds govern financial and business matters; Clubs are the lucky cards; while Spades are the evil ones, governing ill-health, death, financial loss and ruin. They also represent illicit love affairs.

These general meanings should be borne in mind when looking at the type card that represents the enquirer— one suit or the other is sure to be in ascendancy near the type card.

If a number of Court cards run together, it is a sign of much social hospitality or visiting, gaiety of all kinds. Two red Tens coming together foretell a wedding; two red Eights new clothes. A Court card coming between two cards of similar denomination (such as two Tens, two Sevens, etc.) shows that the person represented by the Court card will be involved in legal trouble.

The cards should be cut with the left hand for Divination purposes, and a round table is always preferred ; it is generally believed that the cards do not " tell " so truly when the enquirer spreads them on his own account —in such a case, it is usual to ask some friend to act as intermediary and make the enquiries on the performer's behalf !

Dealing the Cards by Threes

The pack of thirty-two cards is shuffled by the enquirer and cut with the left hand into three heaps. The Diviner takes the centre heap first, places the last heap upon it, and the first cut heap on top of all ; then turning the pack face upwards, he deals off three cards only. If these contain two or more of a suit, the highest in value is withdrawn and placed, face upwards, on the table. The others are thrown face downwards to form a fresh heap.

If the three cards are all of the same value, such as three Kings, three Eights, etc., they are all to be added to those face upwards on the table. When you have gone through the pack in this way, you begin all over again, till either thirteen, fifteen, or seventeen cards are face upwards before you. The card representing the enquirer must always be among these, so if you reach twelve, fourteen, or sixteen without the type card, you must at once pick it from the pack and add it to the end of the row, thus completing the necessary uneven number. The row must always be built from left to right. If the Wish card, the Nine of Hearts, is among these, it is considered a very fortunate sign—the nearer it falls to the type card the greater the chances of prosperity and good fortune.

One card from each end of the row is now to be taken and placed together on the table and their meaning read together, bearing in mind that the card from the right is always the more powerful. Suppose we take the Eight of Spades from the right and the Seven of Clubs from the left, we find that a slight illness or accident will result in the receiving of a small sum of money. On the other hand, if the Seven of Clubs comes from the right and the Eight of Spades from the left, the meaning will be quite different—that the receipt of a small sum of money will result in a slight illness or accident.

In this way all the cards but one are paired off, leaving the " Surprise " card alone, and the reading of this card will affect everything else.

There is another way of working this arrangement, which is only slightly different. The pack having been shuffled and cut into three heaps, the performer takes up the centre heap and removes the bottom card, i.e. the card that is face uppermost. This is placed on the table as the first card of the required row for determining the decrees of Fate. The last cut heap is then similarly dealt with, the bottom card being placed second in the row and the remainder placed on top of the centre heap, as in the first method. So again with the first cut heap, originally on top of the pack.

The cards are now dealt in threes as before, but the highest of each three is chosen quite irrespective of suit. For instance, should you turn up the Seven of Hearts, the Ace of Clubs, and the Jack of Hearts, the Ace would be chosen in this system, whereas the Jack would have been selected under the original method. If three cards of equal value or three cards all of the same suit should appear, all three are added to the row, the card face uppermost being added first, and so on.

Go on in this way till there are only two cards left in your hand, ignoring of course all those thrown away as useless. In the first method the rejected cards are used in order to complete the necessary odd number for the Divination, but that is never done under the present system. Under the original plan, it will often happen that the three cards are all of different suits, and must therefore all be discarded. That is not the case by the present simpler method, as the highest card is chosen each time irrespective of suit. Also you begin with three cards which makes a further difference.

Thus it happens that out of thirty-two cards, you are bound to have *at least* twelve cards in your row, and if you have turned up three of a suit or three of a value at any time, the number will be increased.

Retain the last two cards in your hand and count the cards, face upwards, in your mystic row to see if you have an odd number. If so, discard the two cards left over, and proceed as before to give your Divination by picking up the outside card from each end.

If, however, the number of your row is even, see if the type card (representing the enquirer) is among them ; if not, pick it from the discards and add it to the extreme right of your row. If the type card is already there, see if the Wish card (Nine of Hearts) is also present ; if not, you add it to the end at the right. If both of these are in the row before you, look for the enquirer's Thought card, i.e. the Jack of the same suit as the type card that represents the enquirer.

If all three of these cards are in the row, then add the higher of the two cards remaining in your hand—but if, by any perverse chance, they are both of the same value, then the Fates are not propitious, and the enquirer must come again on some other day, as the row *must* consist of an odd number of cards.

Dealing the Cards by Sevens

After the pack of thirty-two cards has been shuffled by the enquirer and cut with the left hand, the Diviner must count off seven cards, including the top card as the first. The seventh card should be placed face upwards to the left of the table to start the necessary row of cards. Repeat this four times and you will have four odd cards left over. Add these to the discarded cards and let the enquirer well shuffle them and cut as before.

Once again deal them in sevens, taking the seventh card each time as before. This gives you eight cards face upwards on the table. Have the discarded heap once more shuffled and cut and deal as before in sevens, but this time you can only add three cards to the row, as you only have twenty-four left in hand.

When this has been done, place the final three cards, face downwards, by themselves, and make the row of cards exposed on the table up to twelve by adding from the discarded heap either the type card representing the enquirer, the Jack of his suit, to represent his thoughts, or the Nine of Hearts, the Wish card, if either of these is not already in the turned-up row. They must, how-ever, only be taken from the discarded heap—for instance, if the type card is not exposed on the table, and cannot be found among the discards, it is obviously among the three cards left face downwards for the Surprise. It must not be touched, so you must now seek the Jack in the same way—if, for any reason, you cannot thus com-plete the row of twelve, the attempt must be postponed till a more favourable day, or some other method of Divination should be tried.

Some people are very sensitive to odd numbers ; and, if so, the Cards of Fate should be consulted on an odd

day of the month and upon an odd day of the week—
Sunday being the first day in this reckoning. This can
generally be decided by counting the letters in the full
Christian and surnames. Thus the name THOMAS ATKINS
contains twelve letters and therefore an even numbered
day would be more propitious for consulting the cards.

Assuming the row of twelve cards has been completed,
they are paired off as in a previous experiment by taking
one card from either end of the row, the right-hand card
being the active or controlling card of the pair. In the
former experiment, we worked with an odd number of
cards, and that method should be used on odd numbered
days for the benefit of people with odd numbered names.

When working with twelve cards under the present
method, there is no centre card left, of course ; but the
face-down heap of three cards takes its place and is called
the Surprise. Its reading always refers to something
unexpected by the enquirer.

It will be seen that these three methods are all built
on the same general principle—a row of odd or even
number, and the comparison of the end cards of the row,
right with left, together with a strong Surprise at the
finish. All three methods have the advantage of simplicity.

CHAPTER V

AMONG French card-tellers, it is usual to abandon the simple methods used by English tellers when arranging the cards ; instead they use fanciful figures known as Stars. We will give three of these, with full details of their building and reading.

One of the most general methods of laying-out the cards is called the Grand Star, of which we give a diagram. For this purpose all the thirty-two cards of the fortune-telling pack are used—the Deuces, Threes, Fours, Fives, and Sixes are discarded.

A card to represent the enquirer or consultant is selected. If he is a fair man, the King of Hearts is chosen as the card to represent the enquirer. This card is called the significator. If a very fair man or a white-haired man, the card for significator is the King of Diamonds. These two suits are used also for very fair and fair women, the Queen being the significator.

Clubs and Spades represent respectively consultants who are between dark and fair, and very dark persons. Kings and Queens are used for the two sexes. If the enquirer be a widower or widow, Spades is the suit for the significator.

The diagram should now be consulted, in order that the correct mode of laying-out the cards can be seen. First of all the significator is placed on the space numbered

1, and the other cards, in the manner now to be described, placed in proper order upon their correct positions.

After shuffling, first by the operator, and then by the consultant, the cards should be cut with the left hand by the consultant.

When the first cut has been made ten cards are dealt,

THE GRAND STAR

and the eleventh is taken as the first of the lay-out and placed on the space numbered 2 in the diagram. All the remaining cards, thirty in all, are now treated as a pack, cut again by the consultant, and the top card is placed on space No. 3.

Again the cards are treated as a pack, again cut, and the

bottom card of the cut placed on No. 4. This is repeated constantly, taking a card alternately from the top of the bottom half of the cut pack, and from the bottom of the top half of the pack, until sufficient cards have been withdrawn to make up the completed Grand Star.

When, after cutting, the pack is re-made, the top part, which has been cut, should be placed at the bottom of the pack to make it ready for the next cut.

For reading the fortune the cards are taken in pairs, beginning with the outside row of pairs, moving from left to right, contrary clockwise, thus, 14 and 16 ; 21 and 19 ; 15 and 17 ; 20 and 18. The inner circle is next taken in pairs, moving in the opposite direction, from right to left, as a clock's hands go. Thus, 10 and 6 ; 12 and 9 ; 11 and 7 ; 13 and 8. The four centre cards are read in pairs, thus, 4 and 2 ; 5 and 3 ; and the last card, 22, is taken individually. All the cards are read, of course, in special relation to the position each bears to the significator.

Generally, the modifications arising from position are as follows : cards that are directly above the significator show the possibilities of success and achievement. Those directly below denote that which has transpired. To the right of the significator the cards denote that to which the enquirer is approaching, his wishes coming to fulfilment. Those to the left mark obstacles and opposition to be feared.

In addition to these direct positions, there are those that are right and left above, and right and left below, when regarded obliquely. Those to the right above should show helpful signs, to the right below things accomplished towards the desires of the enquirer. To the left above there will appear the obstacles that may arise out of past conditions to thwart the desires, and to the left below those that have already made themselves apparent in the past.

When reading for the Grand Star, some general indications may be gained from groups. Thus, if three or four Kings, Queens, Jacks, or Aces are shown, these will give a general idea that must be taken into consideration in reading the pairs.

As an example of a Grand Star reading, Foli gives the following : " The consultant is represented by the King of Hearts, a fair open-handed, good-natured man, and the pairs come out as follows : Queen of Diamonds and King of Spades (14 and 16) ; Jack of Hearts and Ace of Diamonds (21 and 19).

" Nine of Clubs (reversed) and Queen of Clubs (15 and 17) ; Jack of Spades and Eight of Diamonds (reversed) (20 and 18) ; Ace of Spades and Queen of Spades (6 and 10) ; Jack of Diamonds and King of Clubs (9 and 12) ; Queen of Hearts and Eight of Clubs (8 and 13).

" Nine of Diamonds (reversed) and Jack of Clubs (7 and 11) ; Ace of Hearts and Ten of Spades (4 and 2) ; Nine of Spades and Ten of Hearts (5 and 3) ; the Ace of Clubs is 22.

" Here the consultant is connected with (14) the Queen of Diamonds, a fair woman with a tendency to flirtation ; she is amusing herself with (16) a very dark man, probably a lawyer, of ambitious and not too scrupulous character, who does not wish well to the enquirer.

" The next pair shows the Jack of Hearts, representing Cupid, or the thoughts of the one concerned, linked with (19) Ace of Diamonds, a wedding ring. While this important item is occupying his thoughts he gives a small present, the Nine of Clubs, reversed, to (17) Queen of Clubs, a charming dark lady, who is the real object of his affections.

" The Jack of Spades (20) figuring a legal agent, or the wily lawyer's thoughts, makes mischief, and (18) Eight of Diamonds (reversed) causes the enquirer's love-making to be unsuccessful. (6) Ace of Spades warns him against false friends who will frustrate his matrimonial projects, and in 10 we find one of them, the Queen of Spades, a widow, with possible designs upon him herself.

" The Jack of Diamonds (reversed) (9) shows the mischief maker trying to breed strife with the enquirer's trusty friend (12) King of Clubs, and (8) Queen of Hearts, a fair, lovable woman possessing (13) Eight of Clubs, a dark person's affections. (7) Nine of Diamonds (reversed) tells of a love quarrel owing to (11) Jack of Clubs (reversed) a harmless flirt.

" The enquirer will get (4) the Ace of Hearts, a love letter, but his happiness will be succeeded by (2) Ten of Spades, a card of bad import. (5) The Nine of Spades, tells of grief or sickness, possibly news of a death. But (3) Ten of Hearts, counteracts the evil and promises happiness to the enquirer, who shall triumph over the obstacles in his path and find (22) joy in love in life."

It will be seen here that cards of evil import are made of little avail by their association with those of better omen, and the general indication from the groups is here quite fair.

Another method, known as the Simple Star—see diagram—is with fifteen cards in all. To tell the fortune in this method, place the significator first of all on the centre position marked C (consultant)

Shuffle the cards as previously directed, and let the consultant cut the pack into three. The cards thus cut are to be turned up and used as the basis for the drawing for the Star. From the centre portion of the pack take the first card thus exposed and place it upon 1. From the left-hand portion of the pack take the top card for 2. From the right-hand portion of the pack the card for 3. The fourth card is taken from the centre portion, and so on until twelve have been drawn.

THE SIMPLE STAR

To determine the thirteenth and fourteenth cards, remake the pack, and let the consultant shuffle and cut. Then take the top card of the bottom half for the thirteenth, and the bottom card of the top half for the fourteenth. These should be placed directly upon the significator, as shown in the diagram.

These two cards are very important indications, and

must be read finally as denoting what is likely very soon to come to pass. The general meanings of the card may be used for the reading, with the modifications resulting from the positions as they come out.

Another method recommended by Minetta is called " The Week." First obtain the significator and place this in the centre. Then shuffle the thirty-one remaining cards. Let them be cut by the consultant. Seven cards are then taken in order from the cut, the first being that on the top of the bottom pack.

These seven cards are arranged in a semi-circle over the consultant's card, beginning at the left, somewhat resembling a mushroom with a short stalk ! Each card must then be covered by another. The covering cards, without their faces being seen, may be placed upon those below in any order. The cards are then read in pairs from the left.

An example is given by Sepharial. The first pair were Seven of Spades and Ten of Hearts. This indicates a removal from town. The next were the Ten of Clubs and Eight of Diamonds—a short journey. Next, Seven of Diamonds and Nine of Spades—illness of child or a pet.

Next came Ace of Diamonds and King of Clubs—a letter from a dark man. Next, Eight of Hearts and Nine of Clubs—an invitation to festivities. Next came the Ten of Diamonds and Ace of Clubs—a letter with money ; and finally, the King and Queen of Hearts—the visit of a married couple.

Taken altogether, this is seen to be pretty good. There are only two Spades in the lay-out, and one of these is almost nullified in its evil influence by being in association with a Heart. Without the Heart it might have meant a change or removal, and with evil influences, danger or sickness, for example.

In an ordinary lay-out, if the King of Clubs, representing the consultant, were to appear between the Ace of Diamonds and a Ten of Hearts, the omen is particularly fortunate. It would indicate that the enquirer is on the eve of a very happy marriage. On the contrary, should the cards on either side be the Nine of Spades and the

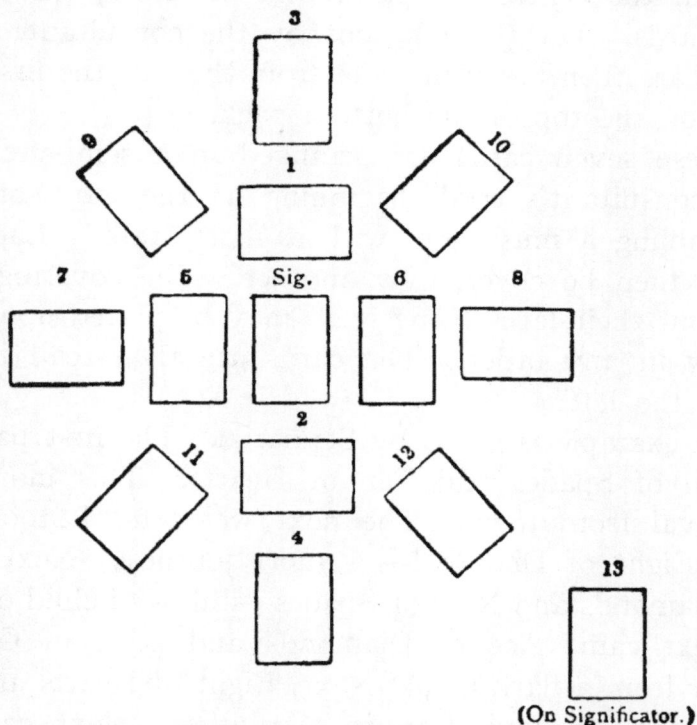

(On Significator.)

THE THIRTEEN CARD STAR

Ace of Spades reversed, very evil results may be looked for. The enquirer is in danger of death, or at least of serious sickness.

Here is another interesting Star, using thirteen cards— for those who believe in the fatalistic powers of the number Thirteen, this method should be adopted.

Place significator, face upwards, on the table. Shuffle the remaining thirty-one cards; cut in three; always take particular notice of the cards exposed at each cut, and watch if, in the deal, they come on or near the significator or the House card, i.e., the Ace of Hearts. If the cards cut are good cards, it is a lucky omen ; if bad cards, there is no doubt that the misfortune cannot be avoided.

Having noted the cards exposed by the cuts, replace the heaps in the original order before you continue.   Place

A TEST READING

two at the head of the significator, two at the feet, two on the right, two on the left, one in each corner, and one on the significator, making in all thirteen cards, in order as shown in diagram.

If the Nine of Hearts comes out in the thirteen, it augurs good luck for the consulter and success to his wishes. Those cards which crown the significator predict the near future ; those at the feet, the past ; those to the left, obstacles ; those to the right, the distant future ; the top corners, present details ; those at the feet, the past details ; the card on the top of the significator, the consolation.   In the example on page 77, the Queen of Diamonds (married) is supposed to be the inquirer.

Crowning the Queen of Diamonds is Eight of Spades, and on that the King of Diamonds ; this predicts a quarrel with her husband.   On her left the Seven of Diamonds and the Ten of Spades ; she has been troubled with the illness of her child.   At her feet the Nine of Diamonds and the Knave of Spades ; the physician has been called in.   On the right the Ten of Hearts and Ten of Clubs ; a change into the country, and recovery of her child. On the Queen the Nine of Hearts ; her troubles are of short duration.

The above method is most useful to ascertain particulars of any business, or even of persons not present.   Always put the card representing the subject on which you want information in the centre, and place the cards round it as already illustrated.   If information is required concerning the house, the Ace of Hearts must be taken from the pack, and used as a significator.   Business is represented by the Ace of Spades ; a journey by the Ten of Clubs ; a child, or animal, by the Seven of Diamonds ; letters or business papers by the Ace of Clubs.

The Star of Fifteen

Take the pack of thirty-two cards and select the type card, placing it face upwards in the centre of the table. The enquirer must now well shuffle the pack and cut it once only with the left hand.   Take the pack and spread it out fan-wise and let the enquirer choose fifteen cards, one by one, placing them one by one, and face downwards, in a heap by themselves.   Discard the remaining cards and pick up the chosen fifteen, holding them face upwards.

Place the first card to the left of the type card, representing the enquirer ; the second card to the right ; the third card goes above, and the fourth below, thus forming

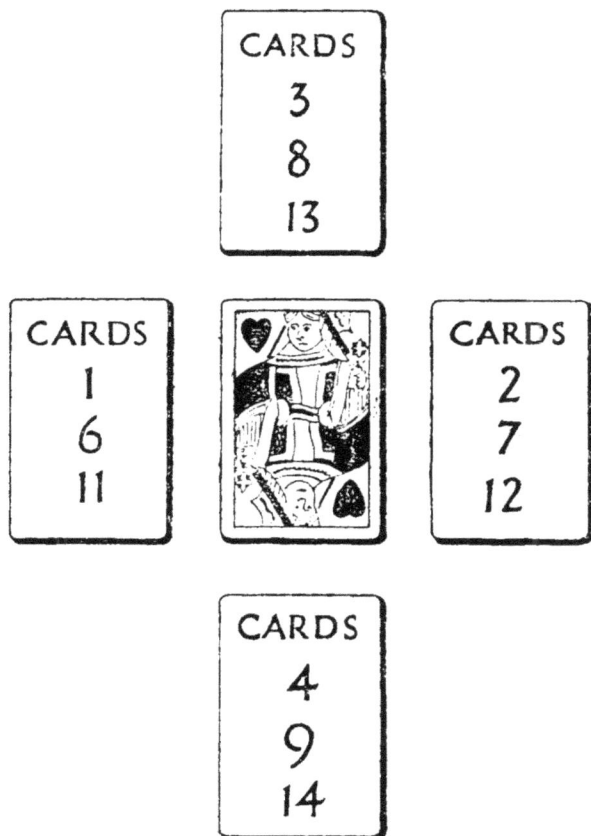

```
        ┌──────────┐
        │  CARDS   │
        │    3     │
        │    8     │
        │    13    │
        └──────────┘

┌──────────┐  ┌──────────┐  ┌──────────┐
│  CARDS   │  │          │  │  CARDS   │
│    1     │  │          │  │    2     │
│    6     │  │          │  │    7     │
│    11    │  │          │  │    12    │
└──────────┘  └──────────┘  └──────────┘

        ┌──────────┐
        │  CARDS   │
        │    4     │
        │    9     │
        │    14    │
        └──────────┘
```

Cards 5, 10 and 15 are placed
upon the centre card of the Star.

THE STAR OF FIFTEEN

a simple cross. The fifth card is now placed upon the type card itself.

Repeat this process with five more cards, thus increasing the size of your cross—and again with the final five cards. The type card will now have three cards on each of the four sides ; while the fifth, tenth, and fifteenth cards will have been placed upon the type card itself, covering it.

Now take each set of three cards by itself and read their meaning according to the table, being specially careful to watch for reversed cards as well as for pairs and triplets. Also carefully note if two or more of the three cards are of any one suit, as that greatly affects the result.

The set of three cards on the left should be read first of all, as they represent the immediate past of the enquirer ; then the set of three on the right which govern the immediate future.

After these, if it is wished, you can read the three cards of the upper set, which show the more remote past and which, consequently, are somewhat affected by your reading of the left-hand set. Balancing one set carefully against the other, you should easily be able to decide if things are improving for your enquirer—or if they are drifting for the reverse.

Now consider the bottom set of three cards, which refer to the more remote future, and, after reading their meaning, noting reverses, pairs, triplets, and suits as before, you must balance these against the right-hand set and thus determine which way the future will tend. Suppose, for instance, that apart from their individual meanings, there are two Spades in the right-hand set and either one or no Spade in the bottom set, then the enquirer may certainly look forward cheerfully to a lessening of any difficulties that may be facing him at the moment.

The central set of three, covering the type card, give your answer to any special wish or question of the enquirer's—they do not apply to the past or future and therefore need not be read as regards their individual meanings. Go by the suit colours, making any necessary allowance for the presence of two or three cards of the same value.

We will conclude these continental methods by giving Monsieur Etteila's fascinating Temple of Fortune, a very

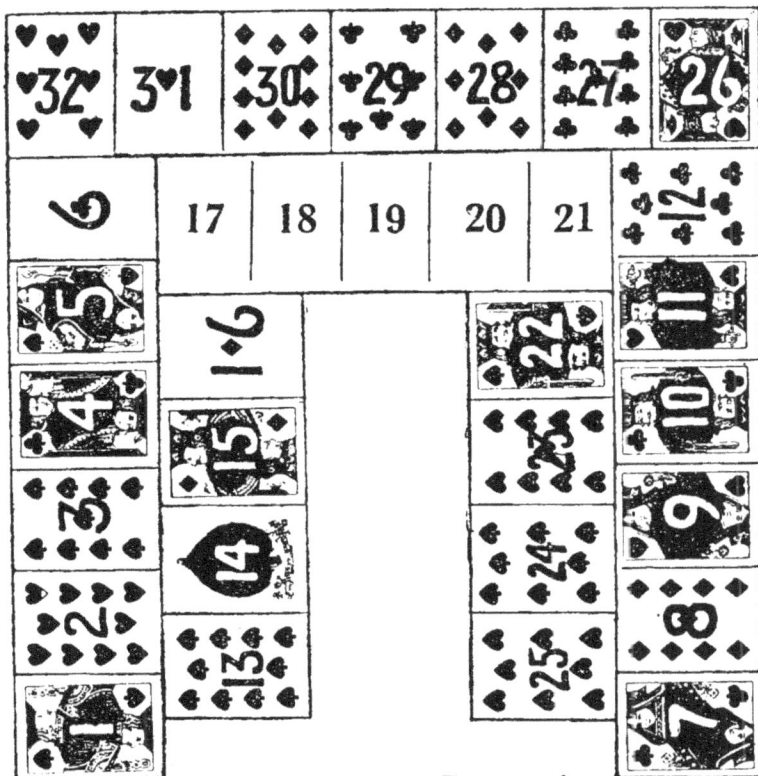

THE TEMPLE OF FORTUNE¡

wonderful system. For this method, the values and meanings of the cards are the same as for Madame Lenormand's system, as given in Chapter II.

The Temple of Fortune is fairly easy to lay out. All the thirty-two cards are used for Etteila's method. They are shuffled finally and cut by the consultant, and laid out in the order shown in diagram.

It will be seen that some of the earliest cards to be

dealt, the first six, with numbers thirteen to sixteen, are those which indicate the past ; the next six with numbers twenty-two to twenty-five indicate the future ; and the last cards to be dealt, with those adjoining them, represent the present.

A further division is suggested. The three inner rows, numbers thirteen to twenty-five, indicate and refer more particularly to the inner life of the consultant, whilst the outer cards represent more specifically his material, worldly, or external affairs.

CHAPTER VI

SOME SIMPLE, BUT EFFECTIVE TELLINGS

THE PAST, PRESENT, AND FUTURE

THE pack of thirty-two cards must be well shuffled by the enquirer and cut with the left hand into two heaps, which can be as equal or unequal in size as the enquirer fancies.

After the cut, the two heaps must not be placed together again until the top card of each has been laid aside, face downwards, to form the usual Surprise. The remaining cards are then squared up and dealt into three heaps of ten cards, which represent respectively the Past (left-hand heap), the Present (centre), and the Future (right-hand heap).

The ten cards of the first heap—the Past—should be spread in a row from left to right and then examined for pairs, triplets, and quadruplets, according to our Table of Meanings. You should carefully note all reversed cards as they tend to lessen the good predicted, or increase the evil, as the case may be. Such cards usually refer to opportunities lost. It is also very helpful to notice which suit predominates in each heap, Clubs being the most fortunate and Spades the most evil. This predominance of colour shows whether the greater amount of success has been reached by the enquirer or is still to come.

After this the cards should be read singly, by their several meanings, from right to left of the row.

When all these have been thrown aside, the centre heap, representing the Present, is similarly examined—and then the Future.

Finally, the Surprise is consulted to see what unexpected event is going to influence the life and fortunes of the enquirer.

THE FOUR ACES

This is a very simple method for determining a single question or wish. The thirty-two cards are well shuffled by the enquirer—the Diviner then deals off thirteen cards, face upwards, on to the table, and makes a careful search for the four Aces. If any are found, place them, face up, by themselves. The remainder of the pack, including what are left of the thirteen, are then re-shuffled as before, and the Diviner again deals out thirteen cards and searches for further Aces.

This can be done for a third time, but that is all. The earlier the four Aces appear, the better it will be for the enquirer—if in the first deal, it is exceptionally fortunate ; if in the second, it is certainly very good luck—as a rule, they are not completed till the third attempt has been made.

Those that appear in each deal should be kept separate, as it is very important to notice the order in which the suits appear. This will clearly show the amount of effort needed before the wish or question is satisfactorily answered—for instance, if the Spade Ace appears first of all, the enquirer must be prepared to face trouble and difficulty, even should all four Aces appear in the course of the first deal.

This is a very useful method to know, as several questions can be dealt with in a very short time, and there is no need to remember any list of meanings. It is as well to limit the questions to three, however, as the cards are never so reliable when overworked, or tired.

Another simple method for answering a single question is worked with the full pack of fifty-two cards. First remove the type card representing the enquirer, King or Queen as it happens to be. Then have the fifty-one cards well shuffled and cut into three heaps of any size. They should be cut towards the right by the left hand—the enquirer makes the first cut, placing the upper portion of the pack on the right and then cuts this latter heap into two.

The Diviner takes the centre heap (originally the middle of the pack) face down in his hand, adds to it the right-hand heap (originally the top of the pack), and finally the left-hand heap goes on top of all. Now make a circle of forty-two cards, face down, on the table—inside this make a triangle of the remaining nine cards.

The enquirer must now turn over any fifteen cards, replacing them, face upwards, in the original positions. When this is done, read them according to the number of each suit exposed.

THE SEVEN ANSWERS

The thirty-two cards are to be shuffled and cut once, as usual with the left hand, and the enquirer should wish once during this process.

Then the cards are dealt out, one by one, so as to form seven heaps—six of these to form a semicircle—the cards for these being placed face downwards, while the seventh heap is built in the centre and the cards are dealt face upwards.

The seven packs represent " yourself " (i.e. the

enquirer); "your home"; "what you expect"; "what you don't expect"; "the Surprise"; "what is sure to come true"; and "your wish."

It will at once be noticed that some heaps will contain five cards each, others only four each. The heaps should be arranged from left to right—the first card dealt starting the heap on the extreme left and the seventh card going, face upwards, in the centre.

Some Diviners employ this method but only use seventeen cards—the pack is shuffled and cut as before, but only the first seventeen cards are dealt. This method is certainly simpler, as the heaps only contain two or three cards each; it is also thought to be a great advantage, as the exposed cards naturally vary greatly as regards the proportion from each suit. If you use the full pack, there must of necessity be eight of each suit; whereas if only seventeen are dealt, six or seven or even eight of one suit might appear on the table, and it is obvious that the preponderance of any suit would greatly affect the reading.

Some Diviners object to the seven packs, maintaining that it is false art to have one heap for " what you don't expect," and another for " the Surprise." The sixth heap is also rather feeble and certainly looks as if it had originally been included to make the number uneven. This School of Diviners therefore deal off thirteen cards only from the full pack of thirty-two, and build up only five heaps for " yourself "; " your home "; " what you expect "; " the Surprise "; and " your wish."

A WEEK'S HAPPENINGS

The enquirer should well shuffle the pack and cut them with the left hand into three heaps, as before explained.

The Diviner now takes the top card of each heap face downwards, and places them so as to start a row of fifteen cards, the top card of the left-hand heap being first removed. The cards are then re-shuffled and cut as before, the Diviner again removing the top card from each heap and adding them to the row. This is repeated five times, so that fifteen cards, face downwards, are ranged on the table from left to right.

The Diviner now turns over, face upwards, the extreme card at either end and reads the meaning which applies to the following day—special importance attaches to the suit colours which will certainly show whether that day will be a fortunate one or not.

In many cases the inner meaning of the cards is never considered at all, this method being used on the Continent to determine, simply and solely, which will be the fortunate and unfortunate days in the week—Sunday counting as the first day, of course. Remember that the right-hand card is the more important—for instance, a Spade on the right and a Club on the left would indicate that things would certainly go wrong in the early part of the day, but would rapidly improve after noon. Whereas a Club on the right and a Spade on the left would indicate a prosperous morning, followed by a calamitous afternoon and evening.

When using this simple form of Divination, no list of meanings has to be consulted, which in many cases is a great advantage; it is therefore an excellent companion method to the one already described for answering questions by the suit colours of the cards turned up.

Fourteen cards are turned up in this way, two and two, leaving the centre card face downwards on the table. The Diviner should now note, on a slip of paper, the point values of each pair of cards, in case the enquirer should be confronted on that day by any business or other matter in which figures are concerned. For instance, if a Nine of Spades and a Seven of Hearts are the cards for the following Tuesday (the third day), then anything involving nine or any multiple of nine should be avoided, and those things involving seven should be followed up. Suppose anyone calls and wishes to make an appointment, fix the seventh, fourteenth, twenty-first, or twenty-eighth day of the month. Should the *seventh day* (i.e. the next Tuesday) fall on the ninth, eighteenth, or twenty-seventh of the month, it would obviously be a bad day to select. In the same way, if the fourteenth, twenty-first, or twenty-eighth of the month was the ninth day following, that also would prove a bad day.

With all these particulars to help him, or her, along, your client should be able to avoid all mishaps and make the best use of the opportunities for good fortune that might come his, or her, way.

The fifteenth card is used to answer one question, which, in this case, must be a spoken one. The suit of the card determines whether the answer is to be " yes " ; " probably " ; " doubtful " ; or " no "—and the pip value should be noted if it can be made to fit in any way, as that particular number will have a fateful influence, one way or another, over the matter in question. Its influence, however, only lasts for the week in question, so if it is a Spade, it is wise to warn your client to delay and wait for a more propitious time before proceeding with the matter in his mind.

THREE QUESTIONS ANSWERED

This is a simple method of Divination that does not require any consultation of Tables of Meanings. The pack of thirty-two cards must be well shuffled by the enquirer and cut into three unequal heaps, using the left hand. That portion of the pack that was previously in the centre is now placed at the bottom ; the top section is placed above this ; and the original bottom section is placed on top.

The cards are now spread out fanwise on the table, face downwards, taking care that every card is visible and that none overlap and hide a neighbouring card. The enquirer must now think of a question, and while doing so should choose three cards and place them, face downwards, on the table.

He, or she, should now think of the second question, and while doing so pick out seven cards, placing them separately on the table, also face downwards. While the third question is being thought of, thirteen cards must be chosen and the remainder of the pack discarded.

The Diviner now turns up the first heap of three cards and determines from these the answer to the question— in this method the lower the value of the cards the less the opposition to the success of the enquirer, the more fortunate the result of his enquiry. The suit colours must also be considered as affecting the result, but the greater importance rests upon the value of the cards— in this case the Ace, of course, is counted as the lowest and most fortunate card in the pack.

Similarly the second heap of seven cards, and the third heap of thirteen, will be turned up, each in its turn, and the answer considered.

This is not only a simple but a quick method of Divination, but obviously it only applies to answers to definite questions.

DIVINATION BY OBSTACLES

Have the pack of thirty-two cards well shuffled and cut once only. Pick out the type card representing the enquirer and hold the rest of the pack face downwards in your hand. The type card is placed in the centre of the table, the top card from the pack is turned over and placed above the type card, the second card being similarly placed below. The third is now placed on the left and the fourth card on the right. The fifth card is placed upon the type card, covering it. The Diviner now discards eight cards altogether, and, that being done, adds another card to each of the five in the same order as before—above, below, left, right, and upon the type card.

Discard eight more cards and place the final five cards as before, one by one, upon the heaps. Read each heap in turn, beginning with the one from above the type card, and only looking out for pairs and triplets, suit colour, and whether the four high cards (the Ace here being counted with the Court cards, as this method is older than the one last described) or the four low cards predominate—the latter being the personal efforts of the enquirer, and the Court cards being the help or interference of other people.

DIVINATION BY PAIRS AND TRIPLETS

This method is not so old as some of the others but is very pretty and effective, besides being reliable.

The pack of thirty-two cards must be well shuffled and cut into three with the left hand, these being arranged as before explained, taking the original centre section for the bottom of the newly arranged pack. The prepared cards are now held in the left hand and the three top cards are turned up. If they contain two or three cards of the same face value or three cards of the same suit, they should be placed face upwards on the table—the others being discarded.

This is repeated till the pack is exhausted, the odd two cards being discarded.

The discarded heap is now well shuffled and cut three times as before—this must always be done by the enquirer and never by the Diviner, who merely deals or arranges the cards and gives their meanings as they appeal to him. Diviners who are slightly clairvoyant make some marvellously accurate predictions without apparently studying the accepted meanings of the cards.

The cards having been shuffled the second time, leaving the selected pairs and triplets face upwards on the table, they are again gone through in sets of three as before in order to increase the row of fateful cards on the table, any odd cards at the end being discarded as at first.

This process is repeated for a third time before the final fateful row of cards is consulted. You can now give a general opinion upon the prospects before the enquirer by a study of the prevailing suits and by noting whether Court cards or plain cards predominate, or you can go further and pick up the cards, two at a time, taking one from each end as in previous methods. This can always be done when cards are arranged in a row, by whatever process they have been selected—always bearing in mind that the right-hand card is more active and positive than the left-hand one.

A very quick, though perhaps rough and ready, method of Divination is to let the enquirer choose thirteen cards haphazard after the pack has been well shuffled and cut once. As chosen, they are placed face upwards across the table from left to right, and the answer to the question is decided by the predominant suits and by the number of Court or plain cards thus selected. Should there be an equal number of cards belonging to two or more suits (obviously with thirteen cards there cannot be an equal number of Court or plain cards), you give preference to that suit that has most cards on the right of the row— these being more active and aggressive.

DIVINATION BY THE SPADE SUIT

The pack must be shuffled and cut into three heaps and rebuilt, as before explained.

The Diviner now holds the pack face upwards in his hand—this is different from most methods of Divination, where the cards are generally dealt from the top of the pack. Each card is looked at, but unless it is a Spade, it is placed on the table, face upwards, to form a fresh pack. As soon as a Spade is reached, that card is also discarded, but the next following card is placed, face upwards, on the table to start the necessary fateful row of cards. Should two or more Spades come together, only the first one is discarded, the other or others being added to the fateful row in front of you, together with the next card following the last of that batch of Spades.

This is continued till the pack is exhausted, when the discarded heap is taken up and treated in the same fashion *without being re-shuffled.*

This process is repeated for a third time, and then the type card must be looked for—if it is not already in the row, it must be found and added at the end. The Diviner now counts the third, seventh, and thirteenth card from the type card, in each case counting the type card as one. These three cards are not removed from the row, but can be pulled down a little below the level of the others, as they form the dominant trio in this method.

This counting is done to the left, and when you reach the extreme card, the one first put on the table, you go back to the end card at the right and so continue your count if necessary. But it often happens that all three dominant cards are reached before you come to the card on the extreme left. Of these three cards, the one finally nearest the right is the most powerful. It clearly depends upon the position in the row of the type card itself whether the third, seventh, or thirteenth is the important card.

It is generally agreed that by this method only near events can be predicted, certainly it does not cover more than a month.

A somewhat similar method is used in England with the full pack, but instead of using the Spade suit as the guide for the cards to be picked out, you go by the points of the cards—the Ace in this method counts as one. The pack having been shuffled and cut into three heaps and rebuilt as before, you deal the cards from the top, placing each one face upwards on the table as you do so. While you do this, you count aloud : one, two, three, four, five, six, seven, eight, nine, ten, Jack, Queen, King, one, etc.

If any card, irrespective of suit, turns up at the proper count—for instance, if the fifth card really is a Five, it is placed as one of the fateful row, and the counting continues as before.

When the pack is exhausted, the discarded cards are turned over and dealt out again as before, turning each one up in the Spade suit method ; but you must be careful after the second time to note at which card you cease calling, as when you start the third deal you do not re-start the counting at one, but continue from where you left off.

In addition to the cards that turn up at their own proper calls, you also add to the fateful row any cards that turn up three or more at a time, whether at their proper call or not. Thus three Tens, three Fives, would be added, merely because they follow each other in value, but three Hearts or three Spades would be ignored, as in this method the dealing takes no account of suits.

The Diviner now forms a rough cross from the cards in the row, placing the first card from the extreme left to form the top of the cross ; the next card to form the bottom of the cross ; the third to form the right, and the fourth the left wings. The next four cards are built above these in the same way—top, bottom, right, left, and so you build the cross till all the chosen cards are used up.

The top heap is read first, as the predictions from those cards are supposed to come first ; then the bottom heap ; then the right and then the left—the latter, of course, being very far into the future. You can allow roughly a fortnight for each heap.

THE DECISION BY ACES

The pack of thirty-two cards must be well shuffled and cut into three and rebuilt. The Diviner now turns up three cards at a time—if an Ace appears among them, or the type card representing the enquirer, or the Wish card (Nine of Hearts), those three cards must be taken out and placed face upwards on the table. This continues till the six cards are all exposed, i.e. the four Aces, type card, and the Wish card. Those sets of three cards not containing one or more of the six fateful cards are to be discarded altogether.

When the necessary cards are obtained, they must be gathered together, re-shuffled and cut and dealt out once more in sets of three, retaining those sets only that contain one or more of the six cards of Fate. This is repeated for a third time—if the six cards are now gathered together within a total of nine cards (or fewer) the Wish will prove successful. If in twelve, the result is doubtful; but if over twelve, the reply is in the negative. If under nine, then the fewer the cards, the quicker and more decisive the result.

The following is the record of an actual test and will show how it works : The type card was the King of Clubs, as a dark man was the enquirer. The first three cards turned up were the King of Diamonds, Ace of Spades, and King of Clubs—these were retained on the table, as they include both an Ace and the type card. The second set were the King of Spades, Queen of Spades, and Ten of Diamonds—these were discarded as useless. The third set were the Ten of Hearts, the Six of Diamonds, and the King of Hearts, and were also discarded. The fourth set were the Seven of Spades, the Eight of Spades, and the Ace of Diamonds, and were kept. The fifth set contained the Nine of Diamonds, Eight of Clubs, and Ace of Clubs, and of course were retained. The sixth set were the Jack of Clubs, Ten of Spades, and Ace of Hearts, and were left on the table; while the seventh set completed the first deal, as it contained the Jack of Spades, Nine of Hearts, and Five of Clubs.

The remainder of the pack, therefore, was added to the discarded heap, and the fifteen cards, face upwards, on the table, were gathered together, well shuffled, and again dealt in sets of three, with the following result : First came the Ace of Spades, Nine of Hearts, and Jack of Spades ; then the Ten of Spades, Ace of Hearts, and Nine of Diamonds. These were followed by the King of Diamonds, Five of Clubs, and Jack of Clubs, and of course, these three cards were at once discarded to the satisfaction of the enquirer. Then came a set consisting of the Seven of Spades, Ace of Diamonds, and Eight of Clubs, which were retained ; and finally, the Eight of Spades, Ace of Clubs, and the King of Clubs, which were also kept.

These twelve cards were now gathered and shuffled for the third and fateful deal, the result of which was as follows : The first set contained the Ace of Hearts, Nine of Hearts, and the King of Clubs—a very good start, giving us three of the necessary cards at once. The second set contained the Nine of Diamonds, Jack of Spades, and Eight of Clubs, indicating some obstacle or difficulty to be faced, as none of these cards were of any use and clearly delayed the gratification of the enquirer's wish. Then came the Ace of Clubs, Ace of Spades, and Ten of Spades, thus destroying all hope of immediate success—but the final set commenced with the Ace of Diamonds, thus enabling us to get out at the tenth card. This is quite good, and shows success after some small delay or difficulty—indeed, it is always reckoned satisfactory if the six fateful cards can be secured at the eleventh. Six or seven would show startling and unexpected good fortune ; eight or nine is extremely fortunate ; ten or eleven quite satisfactory ; twelve or thirteen are very doubtful ; while fourteen or fifteen may be looked upon as a distinct negative.

There is another way of deciding a question by the Aces which is a general favourite and is considered very reliable.

The pack, being well shuffled, is cut once only with the left hand. Thirteen cards are then dealt from the top, face upwards, and if any Aces are among them, they (the Aces only) are retained. The pack is now re-shuffled and cut, and again thirteen cards are dealt and any Aces are removed. This is repeated a third time, and if, in these three deals, the four Aces have all been secured the enquirer may feel satisfied that his wish will be granted.

Should the Aces be secured in the second deal, or in the first (a very rare occurrence), the result naturally will be very much more favourable. But if in the three deals only three Aces are secured, the result is doubtful—whereas if fewer than three turn up, the wish will not be gratified.

There is still another method of working by the Aces—it is rather more elaborate and a favourable result is not so easily obtained. First of all pick out the four Aces, the type card to represent the enquirer, the Nine of Spades to represent disappointment, and a seventh card to represent the question itself—if about money, this would be the Ten of Diamonds ; if about business, then the Ten of Clubs ; if about a woman, then the Queen nearest to her in suit colour ; if about a man, then the corresponding King. For any general wish, choose the Jack of the enquirer's own suit to represent his thoughts.

These seven cards are shuffled but not cut, and are then spread, face downwards, in a row on the table. The remainder of the cards are then well shuffled and cut once and are turned up in a row on the table, seven at a time. The object is to find the Wish card, represented by the Nine of Hearts. Should this card appear in the row of seven, count its position from the left and turn over the corresponding card in the row of fateful cards lying, face downwards, on the table. Should the Nine of Hearts not appear in the first seven cards, repeat the process as before till you come to it.

If the card thus reversed is the Nine of Spades, that settles the enquiry at once by an emphatic negative—if not, the whole performance is repeated and a second card reversed in the fateful row of seven. If the fatal

G

Nine of Spades is once more avoided, the process is repeated for a third time—the appearance of the Disappointment card after the second deal is not, of course, so emphatic as if it is reversed at once, but it is still a negative, though with no attendant disaster or unpleasantness. If it is discovered after the third deal, there is still a chance of success if the enquirer is keen enough to take the necessary trouble over the matter.

The methods given so far are all well known and in universal use, but in the present chapter we have given some very effective methods of Telling, which at the same time are perfectly simple. We wish to draw special attention to the fact that four of these methods can be used at once by the student, as no List of Meanings has to be learnt or studied—these four methods are " The Four Aces " ; " A Week's Happenings " ; " Three Questions Answered " ; and " Decision by Aces."

CHAPTER VII

NAPOLEON'S CARD METHODS

IT is well known that the great Napoleon was very superstitious, and that he had implicit faith in what he termed his Star, or Destiny. In his earlier years his undoubted genius carried all before him, though it is amusing to read—in one of the life stories of the great soldier-emperor—that his mother used to "spank" him in the generous old-fashioned way, merely looking upon him as a wilful and unruly youngster.

The tragic end of his career and of his life was due, without doubt, to the fact that he allowed superstition to swamp reason—he no longer made careful plans, but trusted almost entirely to what we call "luck." It is, however, a fact that he carried with him everywhere a volume that has become known as *Napoleon's Book of Fate* "*—a curious collection of superstitious lore, dealing with such varied subjects as Moles, the Weather, Astrology, Palmistry, Physiognomy, Lucky Days, Dice, Dominoes, Charms, Card Divination, Dreams, and several others.

As this book is very popular, we think it wise to quote in full Napoleon's methods for Fortune Telling by means of the cards.

The order and comparative value of the different suits is as follows : First on the list stand "Clubs," as they

* Published by Foulsham, Limited, London, at Two Shillings.

mostly portend happiness ; and—no matter how numerous or how accompanied—are rarely or never of bad augury. Next come " Hearts," which usually signify joy, liberality, or good temper ; " Diamonds," on the contrary, denote delay, quarrels, and annoyance ; and " Spades "—the worst suit of all—grief, sickness, and loss of money.

We are, of course, speaking generally, as in many cases the position of cards entirely changes their signification— their individual and relative meaning being often widely different. Thus, for example, the King of Hearts, the Nine of Hearts, and the Nine of Clubs, respectively signify —a liberal man, joy, and success in love ; but change their position by placing the King between the two Nines, and you would read that a man, then rich and happy, would be ere long consigned to a prison !

The individual meaning attached to the thirty-two cards employed is as follows :

Ace of Clubs.—Signifies joy, great wealth, or good news. Reversed, the joy will be of brief duration.

King of Clubs.—A frank, liberal, affectionate, upright, and faithful man, fond of serving his friends. Reversed, he will meet with a disappointment.

Queen of Clubs.—An affectionate woman, but quick-tempered, rather amorous, one that will yield her maiden person to a generous lover, happy and loving, will be married. Reversed, jealous and malicious.

Jack of Clubs.—A clever young man, generous and sincere. Reversed, a harmless flirt and flatterer.

Ten of Clubs.—Great wealth, success, or grandeur. Reversed, want of success in some small matter.

Nine of Clubs.—Unexpected gain, or a legacy. Reversed, some trifling present, you will displease your friends.

Eight of Clubs.—Signifies a dark person's affections,

which, if returned, will be the cause of great prosperity. Reversed, those of a fool, and attendant unhappiness if reciprocated.

Seven of Clubs.—Promises a most brilliant fortune, or unexpectedly recovered debt. Reversed, a far smaller amount.

Ace of Hearts.—A love-letter, or some pleasant news. Reversed, a friend's visit.

King of Hearts.—A fair complexion, liberal man. Reversed, will meet with disappointment.

Queen of Hearts.—A mild, amiable woman, a great beauty. Reversed, has been crossed in love.

Jack of Hearts.—A gay young bachelor, who dreams only of pleasure, fond of racing. Reversed, a discontented military man.

Ten of Hearts.—Indicates happiness, triumph. Reversed, some slight anxiety.

Nine of Hearts.—Joy, satisfaction, success, are your delight. Reversed, a passing chagrin.

Eight of Hearts.—A fair person's affections. Reversed, indifference on their part.

Seven of Hearts.—Will be happily married, pleasant thoughts, tranquillity. Reversed, ennui, weariness.

Ace of Diamonds.—Shows a person fond of rural sports, also fond of gardening. It also signifies a letter soon to be received; and if the card be reversed, containing bad news.

King of Diamonds.—A fair man of a fiery temper—generally in the army—but both cunning and dangerous. Reversed, a threatened danger, caused by machinations on his part.

Queen of Diamonds.—An ill-bred, scandal-loving woman, unsteady. Reversed, she is to be greatly feared.

Jack of Diamonds.—A tale-bearing servant, or unfaithful friend. Reversed, will be the cause of mischief and unhappiness.

Ten of Diamonds.—Indicates a husband and wife, with great wealth, many children ; a journey, or change of residence. Reversed, it will not prove fortunate.

Nine of Diamonds.—Annoyance, delay. Reversed, either a family or a love quarrel.

Eight of Diamonds.—Love-making. Reversed, unsuccessful.

Seven of Diamonds.—Declares that you will spend your happiest days in the country, and have uninterrupted happiness. Reversed, implicated in a foolish scandal.

N.B.—In order to know whether the Ace, Ten, Nine, Eight, and Seven of Diamonds are reversed, it is better to make a small pencil mark on each, to show which is the top of the card.

Ace of Spades.—Pleasure. Reversed, grief, bad news.

King of Spades.—An envious man, an enemy, or a dishonest lawyer, who is to be feared. Reversed, impotent malice.

Queen of Spades.—A loving widow. Reversed, a dangerous and malicious woman.

Jack of Spades.—A dark, ill-bred young man. Reversed, he is plotting some mischief.

Ten of Spades.—A card of bad import. Tears, a prison. Reversed, brief affliction.

Nine of Spades.—Tidings of a death. Reversed, it will be some near relative.

Eight of Spades.—The most unlucky card in the pack. Approaching illness. Reversed, a marriage broken off, or offer refused.

Seven of Spades.—Slight annoyances, loss of a friend. Reversed, a foolish intrigue.

The Court cards of Hearts and Diamonds usually represent persons of fair complexion; Clubs and Spades, the opposite.

Four Aces, coming together, or following each other, announce danger, failure in business, and sometimes imprisonment. If one or more of them be reversed the danger will be lessened, but that is all.

Three Aces, coming in the same manner.—Good tidings; if reversed, folly.

Two Aces.—A plot; if reversed, it will not succeed.

Four Kings.—Rewards, dignities, honours; reversed, they will be less, but sooner received.

Three Kings.—A consultation on important business, the result of which will be highly satisfactory; if reversed, success will be doubtful.

Two Kings.—A partnership in business if reversed, a dissolution of the same. Sometimes this only denotes friendly projects.

Four Queens.—Company, society; one or more reversed denote that the entertainment will not go off well.

Three Queens.—Morning calls; reversed a lot of chattering and scandal, or deceit.

Two Queens.—A meeting between friends; reversed, poverty, troubles, in which one will involve the other.

Four Jacks.—A noisy party—mostly young people; reversed, a drinking bout, ending in a quarrel.

Three Jacks.—False friends; reversed, a quarrel with some low person.

Two Jacks.—Evil intentions; reversed, danger.

Four Tens.—Great success in projected enterprises; reversed, the success will not be so brilliant, but still it will be favourable.

Three Tens.—Improper conduct; reversed, failure.

Two Tens.—Change of trade or profession ; reversed, denotes that the prospect is only a distant one.

Four Nines.—A great surprise ; reversed, a public dinner.

Three Nines.—Joy, fortune, health ; reversed, wealth lost by imprudence in marriage.

Two Nines.—A little gain ; reversed, trifling losses at cards.

Four Eights.—A short journey ; reversed, the return of a friend or relative.

Three Eights.—Thoughts of marriage ; reversed, folly, flirtation.

Two Eights.—A brief love-dream ; reversed, small pleasures and trifling pains.

Four Sevens.—Intrigues among servants or low people, threats, snares, and disputes ; reversed, that their malice will be impotent to harm, and that the punishment will fall on themselves.

Three Sevens.—Sickness, premature old age ; reversed, slight and brief indisposition.

Two Sevens.—Levity ; reversed, regret.

Any picture-card between two others of equal value— as two Tens, two Aces, etc.—denotes that the person represented by that card runs the risk of a prison.

It requires no great effort to commit these significations to memory, but it must be remembered that they are but what the alphabet is to the printed book ; a little attention and practice, however, will soon enable the learner to form these mystic letters into words, and words into phrases, in other language, to assemble these cards together and read the events, past and to come, their pictured faces pretend to reveal.

There are several ways of doing this ; but we will give them all, so as to afford our readers an ample choice of methods of prying into futurity.

No. 1.—Dealing the Cards by Threes

First take the pack of thirty-two selected cards (viz. the Ace, King, Queen, Jack, Ten, Nine, Eight, and Seven of each suit), having before fixed upon the one you intend to represent yourself, supposing always you are making the essay on your own behalf. If not, it must represent the person for whom you are acting. In doing this, it is necessary to remember that the card chosen should be according to the complexion of the chooser—King or Queen of Diamonds for a very fair person, the same of Hearts for one rather darker, Clubs for one darker still, and Spades only for one very dark indeed. The card chosen also loses its signification, and simply becomes the representative of a dark or fair man or woman, as the case may be.

Having settled this point, shuffle the cards, and either cut them or have them cut for you (according to whether you are acting for yourself or another person), taking care to use the left hand. That done, turn them up by threes, and every time you find in these triplets two of the same suit—such as two Hearts, two Clubs, etc., withdraw the highest card and place it on the table before you. If the triplet should chance to be all of the same suit, the highest card is still to be the only one withdrawn ; but should it consist of three of the same value but different suits, such as three Kings, etc., they are all to be appropriated. We will suppose that, after having turned up the cards, three by three, you have been able to withdraw six, leaving twenty-six, which you shuffle and cut, and again turn up by threes, acting precisely as you did before, until you have obtained either thirteen, fifteen, or seventeen cards. Recollect that the number must always be uneven, and that the card representing the person for whom the essay is made must make one of it. Even if the requisite thirteen, fifteen, or seventeen have been obtained, and this one has not made its appearance, the operation must be recommenced. Let us suppose the person whose fortune is being read to be a lady, represented by the Queen of Hearts, and that fifteen cards have been obtained and laid out—in the form of a half-circle—in the order they were drawn, viz. the Seven of Clubs, the Ten of Diamonds, the Seven of Hearts, the Jack of Clubs, the King of Diamonds, the Nine of Diamonds, the Ten of Hearts, the Queen of Spades, the Eight of Hearts, the Jack of Diamonds, the Queen of Hearts, the Nine of Clubs, the Seven of Spades, the Ace of Clubs, and the Eight of Spades. Having considered your cards, you will find among them two Queens, two Jacks, two Tens, three Sevens, two Eights, and two Nines; you are, therefore, able to announce:

" The two Queens signify the re-union of friends; the two Jacks, that there is mischief being made between them. These two Tens denote a change of profession, which, from one of them being between two Sevens, I see will not be effected without some difficulty, the cause of which, according to these three Sevens, will be illness. However, these two Nines promise some small gain, resulting—so say these two Eights—from a love affair."

You now begin to count seven cards from right to left, beginning with the Queen of Hearts, who represents the lady you are acting for. The seventh being the King of Diamonds, you may say:

" You often think of a fair man in uniform."

The next seventh card (counting the King of Diamonds as one) proves to be the Ace of Clubs; you add:

" You will receive from him some very joyful tidings; he, besides, intends making you a present."

Count the Ace of Clubs as " one," and proceeding to the next seventh card, the Queen of Spades, you resume:

" A widow is endeavouring to injure you, on this very account ; and " (the seventh card, counting the Queen as one, being the Ten of Diamonds) " the annoyance she gives you will oblige you either to take a journey or change your residence ; but " (the Ten of Diamonds being imprisoned between two Sevens) " your journey or removal will meet with some obstacle."

On proceeding to count as before, calling the Ten of Diamonds one, you will find the seventh card prove to be the Queen of Hearts herself, the person for whom you are acting, and may safely conclude by saying :

" But this you will overcome of yourself, without needing anyone's aid or assistance."

Now take the two cards at either extremity of the half-circle, which are, respectively, the Eight of Spades and the Seven of Clubs, unite them, and continue :

" A sickness, which will lead to your receiving a small sum of money."

Repeat the same manœuvre, which brings together the Ace of Clubs and the Ten of Diamonds.

" Good news, which will make you decide on taking a journey, destined to prove a very happy one, and which will occasion you to receive a sum of money."

The next cards united, being the Seven of Spades and the Seven of Hearts, you say :

" Tranquillity and peace of mind, followed by slight anxiety, quickly succeeded by love and happiness."

Then follows the Nine of Clubs and the Jack of Clubs foretelling :

" You will certainly receive money, through the exertions of a clever dark young man—Queen of Hearts and King of Diamonds—which comes from the fair man in uniform ; this rencontre announces some great happiness in store for you, and complete fulfilment of your wishes—

Jack of Diamonds and Nine of Diamonds—although this happy result will be delayed for a time, through some fair young man, not famed for his delicacy. Eight of Hearts and Ten of Hearts—love, joy, and triumph. The Queen of Spades, who remains alone, is the widow who is endeavouring to injure you, and who finds herself abandoned by all her friends ! "

Now gather up the cards you have been using, shuffle and cut them with the left hand, and proceed to make them into three packs by dealing one to the left, one in the middle, and one to the right ; a fourth is laid aside to form a " Surprise." Then continue to deal the cards to each of the three packs in turn, until their number is exhausted, when it will be found that the left-hand and middle packs contain each five cards, whilst the one on the right hand consists of only four.

Now ask the person consulting you to select one of the three packs. We will suppose this to be the middle one, and that the cards comprising it are the Jack of Diamonds, the King of Diamonds, the Seven of Spades, the Queen of Spades, and the Seven of Clubs. These, by recollecting our previous instructions regarding the individual and relative signification of the cards, are easily interpreted as follows :

" The Jack of Clubs—a fair young man, possessed of no delicacy of feeling, who seeks to injure—the King of Diamonds—a fair man in uniform—Seven of Spades—and will succeed in causing him some annoyance—the Queen of Spades—at the instigation of a spiteful woman—Seven of Clubs—but by means of a small sum of money matters will be finally easily arranged."

Next take up the left-hand pack, which is " for the house "—the former one having been for the lady herself. Supposing it to consist of the Queen of Hearts, the Jack of Clubs, the Eight of Hearts, the Nine of Diamonds, and the Ace of Clubs, they would read thus :

" Queen of Hearts—the lady whose fortune is being told is, or soon will be, in a house—Jack of Clubs—where she will meet with a dark young man, who—Eight of Hearts—will entreat her assistance to forward his interests with a fair girl—Nine of Diamonds—he having met with delays and disappointment—Ace of Clubs—but a letter will arrive announcing the possession of money, which will remove all difficulties."

The third pack is " for those who did not expect it," and will be composed of four cards ; let us say the Ten of Hearts, Nine of Clubs, Eight of Spades, and Ten of Diamonds, signifying—

" The Ten of Hearts—an unexpected piece of good fortune and great happiness—Nine of Clubs—caused by an unlooked-for legacy—Eight of Spades—which joy may perhaps be followed by a slight sickness—Ten of Spades— the result of a fatiguing journey."

There now remains on the table only the card intended for " the Surprise." This, however, must be left un-touched, the other cards gathered up, shuffled, cut, and again laid out in three packs, not forgetting at the first deal to add a card to " the Surprise." After the different packs have been duly examined and explained, as before described, they must again be gathered up, shuffled, etc., indeed, the whole operation repeated, after which the three cards forming " the Surprise " are examined ; and sup-posing them to be the Seven of Hearts, the Jack of Clubs, and the Queen of Spades, are to be thus interpreted :

" Seven of Hearts—pleasant thoughts and friendly in-tentions—Jack of Clubs—of a dark young man—Queen of Spades—relative to a malicious dark woman, or widow, who will cause him much unhappiness."

No. 2.—Dealing the Cards by Sevens

You now shuffle the pack of thirty-two selected cards, which, as we before stated, consist of the Ace, King, Queen, Jack, Ten, Nine, Eight, and Seven, of each suit—either cut them yourself, or, if acting for another person, let that person cut them, taking care to use the left hand. Then count seven cards, beginning with the one lying on the top of the pack. The first six are useless, so put them aside, and retain only the seventh, which is to be placed face uppermost on the table before you. Repeat this three times more, then shuffle and cut the cards you have thrown on one side, together with those remaining in your hand, and tell them out in sevens as before, until you have thus obtained twelve cards. It is, however, indispensable that the one representing the person whose fortune is being told should be among the number ; therefore, the whole opera-tion must be recommenced in case of it not having made its appearance. Your twelve cards being now spread out before you in the order in which they have come to hand, you may begin to explain them as described in the manner of dealing the cards in threes, always bearing in mind both their individual and relative signification. Thus, you first count the cards by sevens, beginning with the one repre-senting the person for whom you are acting, going from right to left. Then take the two cards at either extremity of the line or half-circle, and unite them, and afterwards form the three heaps or packs and " the Surprise " pre-cisely as we have before described. Indeed, the only difference between the two methods is the manner in which the cards are obtained.

No. 3.—Dealing the Cards by Fifteens

After having well shuffled and cut the cards, or, as we have before said, had them cut, deal them out in two packs, containing sixteen cards in each. Desire the person consulting you to choose one of them ; lay aside the first card, to form " the Surprise "; turn up the other fifteen, and range them in a half-circle before you, going from left to right, placing them in the order in which they come to hand, and taking care to remark whether the one representing the person for whom you are acting is among them. If not, the cards must be all gathered up, shuffled, cut, and dealt as before, and this must be repeated until the missing card makes its appearance in the pack chosen by the person it represents. Now proceed to explain them— first, by interpreting the meaning of any pairs, triplets, or quartettes among them ; then by counting them in sevens, going from right to left, and beginning with the card representing the person consulting you ; and lastly, by taking the cards at either extremity of the line and pairing them. This being done, gather up the fifteen cards, shuffle, cut, and deal them so as to form three packs of five cards each. From each of these three packs withdraw the topmost card, and place them on the one laid aside to form " the Surprise," thus forming four packs of four cards each.

Desire the person for whom you are acting to choose one of these packs " for herself," or " himself," as the case may be. Turn it up, and spread out the four cards it contains, from left to right, explaining their individual and relative signification. Next proceed in like manner with the pack on your left hand, which will be " for the house " ; then the third one, " for those who do not expect it " ; and lastly, " the Surprise."

In order to render our meaning perfectly clear, we will give another example. Let us suppose the pack for the person consulting is composed of the Jack of Hearts, the Ace of Diamonds, the Queen of Clubs, and the Eight of Spades reversed. By the aid of the list of meanings we have given it will be easy to interpret them as follows :

" The Jack of Hearts is a gay young bachelor—the Ace of Diamonds—who has written, or will very soon write, a letter—the Queen of Clubs—to a dark woman—Eight of Spades reversed—to make proposals to her, which will not be accepted."

On looking back to the list of significations, it will be found to run thus :

Jack of Hearts—A gay young bachelor, who thinks only of pleasure.

Ace of Diamonds.—A letter, soon to be received.

Queen of Clubs.—An affectionate woman, but quick-tempered and touchy.

Eight of Spades.—If reversed, a marriage broken off, or, offer refused.

It will thus be seen that each card forms, as it were, a phrase, from an assemblage of which nothing but a little practice is required to form complete sentences. Of this we will give a further example, by interpreting the signification of the three other packs—" for the house," " for those who do not expect it," and " the Surprise." The first of these, " for the house," we will suppose to consist of the Queen of Hearts, the Jack of Spades reversed, the Ace of Clubs, and the Nine of Diamonds, which reads thus :

" The Queen of Hearts is a fair woman, mild and amiable in disposition, who—Jack of Spades reversed—will be deceived by a dark, ill-bred young man—the Ace of Clubs—but she will receive some good news, which will console her—Nine of Diamonds—although it is probable that the news may be delayed."

The pack " for those who do not expect it," consisting of the Queen of Diamonds, the King of Spades, the Ace of Hearts reversed, and the Seven of Spades, would signify :

" The Queen of Diamonds is a mischief-making woman —the King of Spades—who is in league with a dishonest lawyer—Ace of Hearts reversed—they will hold a consultation together—Seven of Spades—but the harm they will do will soon be repaired."

Last comes " the Surprise," formed by, we will suppose, the Jack of Clubs, the Ten of Diamonds, the Queen of Spades, and the Nine of Spades, of which the interpretation is :

" The Jack of Clubs is a clever, enterprising young man— Ten of Diamonds—about to undertake a journey—Queen of Spades—for the purpose of visiting a widow—Nine of Spades—but one or both of their lives will be endangered."

No. 4.—The Twenty-one Cards

After having shuffled the thirty-two cards, and cut, or had them cut, with the left hand, withdraw from the pack the first eleven, and lay them on one side. The remainder— twenty-one in all—are to be shuffled again and cut. That done, lay the topmost card on one side to form " the Surprise," and range the remaining twenty before you, in the order in which they come to hand. Then see whether the card representing the person consulting you is among them; if not, one must be withdrawn from the eleven useless ones, and placed at the right extremity of the row—where it represents the missing card, no matter what it may really be. We will, however, suppose that the person wishing to make the essay is an officer in the army, and consequently

H

represented by the King of Diamonds, and that the twenty cards ranged before you are—the Queen of Diamonds, the King of Clubs, the Ten of Hearts, the Ace of Spades, the Queen of Hearts reversed, the Seven of Spades, the Jack of Diamonds, the Ten of Clubs, the King of Spades, the Eight of Diamonds, the King of Hearts, the Nine of Clubs, the Jack of Spades reversed, the Seven of Hearts, the Ten of Spades, the King of Diamonds, the Ace of Diamonds, the Seven of Clubs, the Nine of Hearts, the Ace of Clubs. You now proceed to examine the cards as they lie, and perceiving that all the four Kings are there, you can predict that great rewards await the person consulting you, and that he will gain great dignity and honour. The two Queens, one of them reversed, announce the re-union of two sorrowful friends ; the three Aces foretell good news ; the three Jacks, one of them reversed, quarrels with some low person ; the three Tens, improper conduct.

You now explain the cards, commencing with the first on the left hand, viz. the Queen of Diamonds : " The Queen of Diamonds is a mischief-making, underbred woman—the King of Clubs—endeavouring to win the affections of a worthy and estimable man—Ten of Hearts —over whose scruples she will triumph. Ace of Spades— The affair will make some noise—Queen of Hearts reversed —and greatly distress a charming fair woman who loves him—Seven of Spades—but her grief will not be of long duration. Jack of Diamonds—An unfaithful servant— Ten of Clubs—will make away with a considerable sum of money—King of Spades—and will be brought to trial— Eight of Diamonds—but saved from punishment through a woman's agency. King of Hearts—A fair man of liberal disposition—Nine of Clubs—will receive a large sum of money—Jack of Spades reversed—which will expose him to the malice of a dark youth of coarse manners. Seven of Hearts—Pleasant thoughts, followed by—Ten of Spades —great chagrin—King of Diamonds—await a man in uniform, who is the person consulting me—Ace of Diamonds —but a letter he will speedily receive—Seven of Clubs— containing a small sum of money—Nine of Hearts—will restore his good spirits—Ace of Clubs—which will be further augmented by some good news." Now turn up "the Surprise"—which we will suppose to prove the Ace of Hearts—" a card that predicts great happiness, caused by a love-letter, but which making up the four Aces shows that this sudden joy will be followed by great misfortunes."

Now gather up the cards, shuffle, cut, and form into three packs, at the first deal laying one aside to form " the Surprise." By the time they are all dealt out it will be found that the two first packets are each composed of seven cards, whilst the third contains only six.

Desire the person consulting you to select one of these, take it up, and spread out the cards, from left to right, explaining them as before described.

Gather up the cards again, shuffle, cut, form into three packs (dealing one card to the Surprise), and proceed as before. Repeat the whole operation once more ; then take up the three cards forming the Surprise, and give their interpretation.

We may remark that no matter how the cards are dealt, whether in threes, sevens, fifteens, or twenty-one, when those lower than the Jack predominate, it foretells success ; if Clubs are the most numerous, they predict gain, consider-able fortune, etc. ; if picture-cards, dignity and honour ; Hearts, gladness, good news ; Spades, death or sickness. These significations are necessarily very vague, and must of course be governed by the position of the cards.

CHAPTER VIII

SOME UNUSUAL METHODS OF TELLING

QUITE recently we came across a little-known method of card-telling, and as it is both simple and fascinating, we obtained permission to publish it and explain the working.

The full pack of cards is used, and must be thoroughly shuffled by the enquirer—we were interested in hearing that this method can be used for indicating our own immediate future, though this is forbidden, or at least discouraged, in most other systems of working the cards.

THE LUNAR SYSTEM OF TELLING

After the pack has been thoroughly mixed, the name of the bottom card should be noted on paper for reference, as this card acts the part of " Significator "—in other words, it represents the enquirer. Then the pack must be cut once, with the left hand, and the exposed card should also be noted—this card represents the thoughts, wish, or most important matter in which the enquirer is interested. This can of course be anything, from a business deal, a love affair, to the serious illness of a friend, or of oneself.

The cut portion of the pack must now be replaced, so that the original bottom card retains this position. Then seven cards are dealt, one by one face upwards, so as to form a row on the table—these cards run from left to right. Now lay out three other similar rows, each one below the preceding row, thus leaving a roughly squared figure of twenty-eight cards.

Now comes the part that needs a little care and thought, but when understood, it is really quite simple. The rough square represents a lunar month, beyond which the cards will not guide you, and nothing can be done in the way of divination unless you can fix the position of the two cards exposed when the pack was cut—as already explained, the first of these represents the Enquirer, and the second his or her Thoughts.

Glance carefully over the exposed cards and see if either or both of these " personal " cards have been exposed in the lunar square. If you are fortunate, and both personal cards are shown on the table, you can at once make your decision in the way to be explained later.

But if you find only one personal card exposed, you are allowed to continue the preparation, in the hope that the second card will turn up before you read what the cards foretell.

You must note the row in which you find the one personal card, because that particular row must not be touched, nor any row above it. So if this personal card falls in the bottom row, you can do no more, and must " read " the cards as they lie on the table. If, however, it is in the third row from the top, this would leave the bottom row free to be altered ; if in the second row, you would have the two bottom rows at your disposal ; while if it falls in the top row, then you can change the following twenty-one cards.

Whatever it may be, one, two, or three rows, you take up the *unused* portion of the pack and place extra cards upon the already exposed cards on the table, and go on to the twenty-eighth card. To make this clear, suppose one personal card is shown in the top row of the original deal. You now commence on the first card of the second row, and distribute twenty-one cards, thus covering all the three lower rows. This leaves only three cards in hand, so whatever happens you cannot go further, and would have to read the cards as they lie, with only one personal card to guide you, unless the second has now been exposed. But in most cases, when one personal card is exposed in the top row, its companion will appear during this second delivery of the cards.

Now suppose the one personal card is shown in the second row of the original lay-out. You now start covering, by placing a fresh card from the unused portion of the pack on to the first card of the third row, and continue to the end of the square. This means the addition of fourteen cards, but still leaves only twenty-eight cards exposed. It is quite probable that the second personal card will now be visible, in which case your preparation is complete, and you read the cards as we shall explain.

But if by chance the second personal card is not then shown, you are allowed a third attempt. But you must be careful to remember that you only have ten cards in hand now, and you *must* cover whole rows at a time or none at all. So in this case, instead of starting with the first card of the third row, you leave that row intact, and place a fresh card on the first place in the bottom row. This again leaves you with three cards in hand, and you proceed to your divination, as before explained, whether the second personal card is exposed or not.

If the one exposed personal card is in the third row of the original square you can of course only recover the bottom row, which you proceed to do. When you have added seven cards, see if the second personal card is now exposed ; if it is, you stop and give your reading. If not, you deal out seven more cards and again examine them. Obviously you can do this three times, when you have only the one row to work upon, but naturally you stop as soon as the required card is seen, though you must be very careful to complete the covering of the entire row.

To make this quite clear, we repeat that whether you have one, two, or three rows to cover, you must go on dealing fresh cards right to the last card, the twenty-eighth of the lunar square. According to chance, you will always have three, ten, seventeen, or twenty-four cards in the unused portion of the pack.

To give your divination from the final square of exposed cards, you treat each card *as one day*, though in actual experience this is not exactly accurate, as it frequently happens that the result comes gradually, not all of a sudden.

Pay particular attention to the cards that lie between the two personal cards—your decision depends upon the suits, and upon whether the cards are Court cards or commoners. For this method of **divination** the Red **cards** are favourable, and the Black **cards** bad. But Hearts are more powerful than Diamonds, while Clubs are nothing like so bad as Spades.

Suppose, for instance, you find four Red cards between the two personal cards : your decision would at once be favourable, and the greater the sequence of unbroken Red cards, the more favourable the result. Naturally you would study the suits before making your decision, because three unbroken Hearts would be quite as good as four Diamonds —in some cases more so.

On the other hand, a sequence of unbroken Black cards will certainly mean No ! Here again you must study the number of the sequence and the suits. For instance, the appearance of two or three Clubs, without Spades, might place the result beyond the time limit of the lunar square, without necessarily indicating a final unsatisfactory result.

In that case you can only advise your client to go on hoping and working to his end, as nothing will come his way for the next four weeks. You can offer to consult the cards again for him or her, but not under fourteen days.

If only one personal card is exposed in the lunar square, you study the cards from that to the final card, explaining that the decision will be delayed over the four weeks, and that a fresh consultation of the cards in a fortnight's time will help to clear matters up. Meanwhile the suits of the cards following the personal card will enable you to encourage or discourage your enquirer.

If neither of the personal cards is shown, you can give no decision either way—the cards must be consulted again or the decision accepted as a negative or unfavourable one.

Apart from the question of suits, you must also study the values of the cards. The Court cards represent people, the King and Queen being male and female friends, the Jacks business acquaintances or strangers, if the matter is purely personal.

You must also remember that the higher commoner cards, Six, Seven, Eight, Nine and Ten, are more powerful for good or for evil than the lower cards, Two, Three, Four and Five. The Ace is always very powerful.

There is one other point for consideration, and this applies to cases where there are a large number of cards between the two personal cards, or alternatively when only one personal card is exposed. You are allowed to cancel cards in couples, under certain conditions. For instance, a Heart can cancel a corresponding Spade, or a Diamond cancel a Club, but the Court cards and Aces are not to be touched. You can pair either a Two, Three, Four or Five with any other of the same series ; or a Six, Seven, Eight, Nine or Ten with any other of that particular series, subject to the rule as to Suit values.

Thus a Two of Hearts and a Five of Spades can be paired and both cards are then removed from the lunar square. together with any cards underneath them, in case you have formed the row more than once. In the same way, from the higher series, you can pair a Ten of Diamonds with an Eight of Clubs, and so on—*any* of the higher Diamonds can be paired with *any* of the higher Clubs, the Hearts with the Spades—*any* of the lower Diamonds with any of the lower Clubs, the Hearts with the Spades.

The importance of this pairing, together with the removal of all cards affected, will be found far greater in actual practice than it may appear on paper. Suppose, for instance, that you have both personal cards exposed, with nine other cards between them, seven of these being Red cards and two Black. If by good fortune you can pair the two Black cards with two Red cards you will have an unbroken series of *five Red cards*. This is not quite so fortunate as an *original* sequence of f ve Red cards, but it shows that all obstacles *can* be overcome, and that is the important point.

In the same way if the colours had been reversed you would be faced with a series of five Black cards—far more difficult to overcome than the original series of seven Black and two Red cards !

This Lunar Square system is so fascinating and clever, as well as being very reliable, that we strongly recommend a careful study of its rules—it has the additional merit of being known only to a few.

SEPHARIAL'S METHOD

This method is based upon the Chaldean science of Horoscopy, and employs the Twelve Celestial Houses or Signs as a means of interpretation, together with four central positions which indicate the immediate surroundings, and one card on the top of the Significator.

The order in which the thirty-two cards are dealt out, after being shuffled and cut to three packs, is represented in the following diagram.

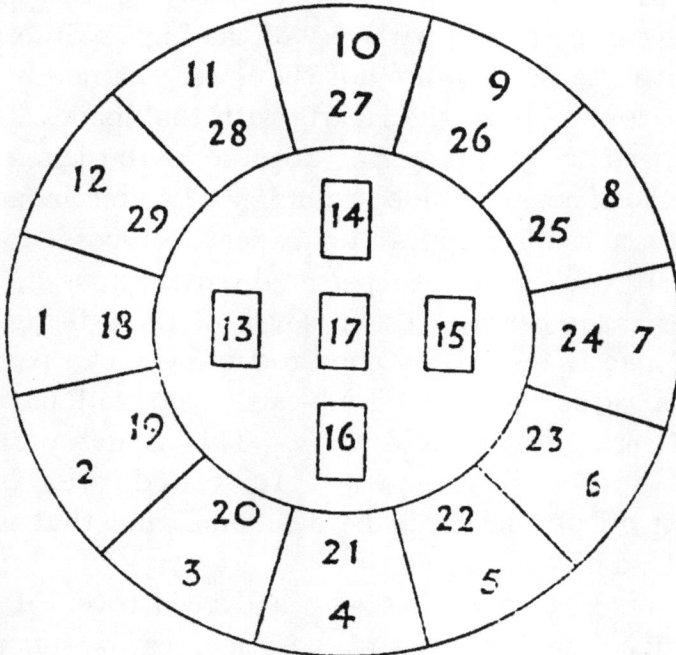

SEPHARIAL'S METHOD

Imagine the Significator to be in the centre. Deal out the cards in the order indicated by the numbers 1 to 29. You will have three cards left over.

INTERPRETATION

Nos. 1 and 18 signify the personal condition of the consultant—his health, mental state, what affects him for good or evil as regards his person.

2 and 19 will show by what means he will gain or lose; his money matters.

3 and 20 show his letters and short journeys, his neighbours and relatives.

4 and 21 show the house and the father.

5 and 22 will show the children, the pleasures, and domestic affairs.

6 and 23 will show the servants and physical comforts of the consultant.

7 and 24 show the marriage condition, and what will help or hinder therein.

8 and 25 will show the wife's financial condition, and any legacies that may fall to the consultant.

9 and 26 will show the long journeys or voyages, news from abroad or foreign affairs, as well as the marriage relatives.

10 and 27 will show the occupation, the mother, and the position of the consultant, and what will help or hinder it.

11 and 28 show the friends and associates.

12 and 29 show enemies, losses, disappointments, and restraints.

13, 14, 15, 16 and 17 will show what immediately surrounds the consultant.

30, 31, and 32 show the end of the matter if the inquiry be on a single point ; but in general they show in what direction the balance of fortune lies, and who shall control the destiny to make or mar it.

If the Ace of Diamonds falls in the 13th place, the Ace of Clubs in the 14th, the Ace of Hearts in the 15th, and the Ace of Spades in the 16th, it is a remarkable augury of a high destiny and great good fortune. Similarly, if the Aces fall in the 1st, 10th, 7th, or 4th places, supported by other good cards. These positions are called the Angles. And if good cards are there the destiny will be remarkable and successful. But if Spades and evil combinations occupy the angles, then the consultant is advised to link his fortunes with those of a more fortunate person, either by marriage or by service, as best he may.

Now observe that the Ace of Diamonds is well placed in the 1st position, the Ten of Diamonds in the 10th place, the Ace of Clubs in the 10th place, the Ten of Clubs in the 7th place, the Ace of Hearts in the 7th place, the Ten of Hearts in the 4th place, the Ace of Spades in the 4th place, the Ten of Spades in the 1st place. All these are good positions, and augur good fortune and an honourable career.

When Kings occupy the angles the destiny is set in high places. When Queens are there it shows the enquirer to be too much under the sway of women and liable to scandal. When Jacks, it portends a dishonourable fame. The Tens or Aces are good in the angles. If the wish card holds the 1st or 10th place, the consultant will gain his greatest wish. If in the 7th place, it will come through marriage. If in the 4th, by inheritance and nearer the end of life.

The Nine of Spades is uniformly evil unless falling with the Ten of Hearts, when it is in a measure corrected.

Great good may be expected from that quarter wherein the Ten of Hearts and the Ace of Clubs or Diamonds shall fall; as if in the 7th House, from the wife; in the 11th, friends; in the 3rd, relatives; in the 10th, business; and so forth.

The Ace of Spades and the Nine of Diamonds show accidents when falling in the 1st or 10th place. The Ace of Spades and Nine of Spades show heavy losses. The Ace of Spades and Ten of Spades show great grief and bereavement, and if it falls in the 4th or 10th place it shows the death of parents; in the 7th, of the wife; and so on.

DEALING THE CARDS BY SIXTEENS

After the thirty-two cards have been well shuffled and cut by the enquirer, they are dealt out into two packs of sixteen cards each, and the enquirer must choose one of these. The top card is now removed, face downwards, and placed by itself on the table.

The other fifteen are turned up and ranged in order from left to right in front of the diviner. The type card, representing the enquirer, *must* be among them—if it is not there, all the cards must be gathered up, re-shuffled and cut, and the preliminary process must be repeated. This goes on till the type card appears among the fifteen in the row.

The reading is given in two ways—first by noting any pairs, triplets, or quartettes among them, giving the meaning from the Table given for the English system. They should then be consulted in pairs as before, by taking one card from each end of the row, leaving a fateful master-card for the finish. This card, as in a former experiment, has more force than any of the seven pairs.

When this has been done, the *fifteen* cards are gathered together and well shuffled, and then dealt so as to form three packs of five cards each. The top card from each heap is then taken and added to the single face-down card to form the Surprise. Thus we get four packs of four cards each.

The enquirer now chooses one of the three heaps—he must not touch the Surprise heap—and this is read as applying to him- or her- self. Of the two remaining heaps, the left-hand one affects the home and the right-hand one covers " some one else " closely connected with the enquirer.

Finally there is the Surprise, which represents something unexpected at the moment by the enquirer.

SOME ITALIAN METHODS

The pack of thirty-two cards are well shuffled and cut once. The present method is dependent upon the suit

colours, and the diviner goes through the pack, turning up
three cards at a time. Should all three be of one suit, they
are placed face upwards on the table, forming the usual
row from left to right. If only two of a suit come together,
the higher card in face value is added to the row and the
other is rejected. If all three cards are of different suits,
all are rejected.

When the pack has been dealt with in this manner, the
rejected cards are re-shuffled, cut, and dealt for a second
time in threes. This is repeated till fifteen cards are in the
row. It is, however, absolutely necessary that the type
card, representing the enquirer, should be in the row, and
if it appears among the fifteen all is well so far. If, however,
it is not in the row, the process of dealing in threes and
adding to the row must be repeated till the type card is
secured—this shows difficulties and troubles and worries
for the enquirer, according to the number of cards added in
this way. Should there be more than fifteen cards in the
completed row, retain only the necessary number, counting
from the extreme right, which in most cases would of course
be the type card itself—unless it made its appearance as
one of a set of three cards of a suit, in which case (all three
having to be added to the row) one or two other cards
might be on the right of the type card.

The row having thus been reduced to fifteen cards, pair
them off, one from each end, as in previous methods, taking
the last (or centre) card as the dominant or Surprise. Now
have the fifteen cards shuffled, and cut and deal them,
one by one, into five heaps of three cards. These should be
read separately, the heap on the left being for the enquirer
himself, the second for the home, the third for the expected,
the fourth for the unexpected, and the fifth for a consolation.

Another Italian method is to sort the cards into suits,
face upwards on the table—each suit forming a separate

row. The pack must be well shuffled and cut into three and rebuilt as already described. Then, beginning with the top card, form your rows, taking care that the suit that first appears is placed to form the top row, and so with each of the others. Go on laying out the cards like this until you reach either the type card representing the enquirer ; or the Wish card, the Nine of Hearts ; or the Disappointment card, the Nine of Spades. Whichever of these three cards appears first is added to the proper row, and this part is now complete, the remainder of the pack being discarded as useless.

Your reading is now given by the general appearance of the cards on the table, and depends very largely upon your experience and judgment—you must note carefully which card was the last added, because if this was the Nine of Spades, it fatally affects everything. You must also be guided by the order of the suits as they lie on the table—the top row being most powerful and also the nearest in point of time. The meaning of each row should be read separately.

THE FATEFUL TWENTY-ONE CARDS

The pack of thirty-two cards must be well shuffled and cut with the left hand. The diviner then takes off the first eleven cards, from the top of the pack, and places them on one side. From the remaining twenty-one cards he takes the uppermost and places it, still face downwards, on the table.

The diviner must now satisfy himself that the type card representing the enquirer is among the twenty cards in his hand, otherwise the full pack must be gathered together once more, re-shuffled and cut, and the proceedings begun all over again, till this essential card is among the fateful twenty.

He now deals these into three heaps, face downwards, and asks the enquirer to choose one of those packs. These must be exposed on the table, face upwards and one by one, beginning by placing the top card on the extreme left. They should now be " read " by their inner meanings, according to the Table given, and the names of the cards, six to seven as it may be, should be noted down on paper. The whole pack is now gathered up again with the exception of the card placed aside for the Surprise, and the whole process is repeated, taking care as before that the enquirer's type card is among the twenty retained for dealing into the three necessary heaps—the top card of the twenty-one being added to the Surprise as with the first deal.

The whole thing is repeated for a third time, so as to cover the immediate past, the present, and the immediate future. You will, after each deal, have made a note of the cards contained in each of the three chosen heaps, and these, however many their number, should now be picked out and arranged in three groups ; one of these containing the cards that only appeared once, another those that appeared twice, and finally those important and fateful cards (if any) that appeared in all three of the chosen heaps.

These should be looked through again for any pairs, triplets, or quadruplets and their meaning read from the Table given. And finally the diviner should study the suit colours in each of these groups, which represent respectively the small affairs, the more important happenings and the really serious events that face the enquirer. But it does not often happen that the same card reappears in all three of the chosen packs.

There is still the Surprise to read and that, naturally, governs something unexpected—in this case also pairs and triplets should be noted, and also the important suit colours.

This is a very thorough method of divination by cards, but it occasionally takes time, as it is quite useless unless the enquirer's type card is among the twenty cards left over for dealing into the three heaps. It need not, of course, be in the chosen heap, and though it must of necessity be among the important twenty after each deal, it frequently happens that it makes no appearance at all in any of the three chosen heaps.

It is considered very important that the diviner should not see the Surprise cards before they are finally exposed on the table, but of course the type card might easily find its way to this heap. When therefore the diviner satisfies himself that the type card is not among the twenty left in his hand he should examine the eleven cards (or ten or nine after the second and third shuffles respectively) that have been discarded and make certain that it really is still in play.

Should the Type card go to the Surprise, the attempt must be given up as hopeless—and, as before stated, nine days must elapse before the cards are consulted again for the same enquirer.

In a trial divination just completed, the following cards appeared in the three selected heaps :

Diamonds : Nine and Jack once only ; Seven, Eight, and Ace twice.
Clubs : Eight and Nine once only ; Seven and Ace twice.
Spades : Ten and Ace once only ; Queen in all three heaps.
Hearts : Nine and King once only.

It will at once be seen that the Nine of Hearts, the Wish card, is among the number, but only appeared once, while the Heart suit is very poorly represented by two cards only out of fourteen. There is very little chance of success,

I

therefore, and the Spade Queen seems to dominate the position. If there had been more Clubs than Diamonds it would have greatly helped matters for the enquirer ; but Diamonds are only the third suit as regards good fortune and are obviously not strong enough to fight successfully against the Spades.

There are three Aces, but one of them is of the fateful Spade suit, though against this is the fact that the Club and Diamond Aces each appeared twice over, which greatly strengthens their influence. But the Ace of Spades, symbol of Death or Disaster, is always an extremely sinister and powerful card, and its power here is enhanced by the trebly occurring Queen of the same suit. It looks as if great good fortune (the Aces) would just be lost, through the influence of a dark woman. This malevolent influence may not be in the enquirer's own life—the woman may control one of those with whom the enquirer is working.

Again the three Nines are a good sign, but they only appear once each, thus clearly showing some *small* gain in place of the much more powerful good fortune that should have come from the Aces. The two Sevens, each appearing twice, and the two Eights strongly confirm the reading and show that good fortune was allowed to slip pass unheeded.

THE FATEFUL SQUARE OF SEVENS

This method of divination dates from the seventeenth century, and has been reprinted several times of recent years, and much praised for its accuracy, apart from its very original character in the building of the design. It is an excellent one, and very reliable, but care must be taken in building up the necessary cards for the experiment —in this case also our diagram should be copied and used.

This method obviously requires the full pack of fifty-two
cards, which must be shuffled well and cut. The enquirer
must now choose three cards haphazard and without looking at them. These should be placed apart on the table.
The remaining forty-nine cards must now be re-shuffled
but not cut.

The diviner now begins to build his square of sevens,
laying the cards face upwards on the table as shown in the
diagram—thus the first card forms the first in the top row,
but the second forms the second in the second row, and
so on down to the seventh, or extreme right-hand card of
the seventh row. When these have been carefully laid out,
the remaining cards must be re-shuffled and a further set
of six cards laid out, above the original seven and working
upwards instead of downwards—these cards are marked
8 to 13 on our diagram. These must be taken from the
bottom of the pack. Once more shuffle and lay out the next
six cards, numbers 14 to 19, working downwards, and
taking them from the top of the pack once more. This
process is repeated till the square is completed, being careful
to re-shuffle after each line of cards is laid out, taking from
the top of the pack when you have to place the cards
downwards and from the bottom of the pack when you
build upwards.

You now have your complete square of sevens, and should
consider the cards carefully, as you must now reduce it to
three cards in a row—the rows counting downwards. Take,
therefore, the extreme right-hand card of the top row and
place it upon the nearest card of the same suit to its left.
If there are other cards of the same suit you now place
these two cards upon them, one by one, always working
to the left—but bear in mind that, whatever its suit may
be, the extreme left card must never be covered. In this
way build all that suit upon each other, the original card

from the extreme right remaining on top—all cards thus covered are to be ignored, but they need not be removed. It makes no difference if you prefer to get rid of them at once—it is merely a matter of convenience. Should there be no other cards of its suit in the row, the extreme right card is left in its place.

You now consider the second card from the right of the top row in the same way, and thus reduce the row of seven cards to one representative of each suit—bearing in mind that the card on the extreme left (the Master Card, as it is called) must never be covered. It follows therefore that when this process is completed you cannot have more than five cards left in each row, one of each suit and the Master Card, and may, indeed, only have two cards, should all be of one suit, a very rare occurrence. This process is, as indicated, applied to each of the seven rows, when you now reduce your figure to its final fateful shape by throwing away all cards beyond three, counting from the Master Card and retaining the next *two* cards on the right. In the very rare event of all cards (excluding the Master Card) being of one suit in a row, you would obviously only have two in that particular row—this makes no difference and must not be interfered with.

You now have a mystic figure, consisting of seven rows of three cards, and from these you give your reading. Note first of all whether there are more red cards than black, as the red aspect is considered favourable. You must, however, bear in mind that Clubs are the most fortunate suit of all, and should these form the bulk of the black cards, they would be amply sufficient to sustain the red favourable aspect, even if there should be a slight black majority. They are held to represent the Intellect and Judgment, as the Hearts govern the Affections and Passions—while the Diamonds represent Money and out-

1	13	24	33	40	45	48
14	2	12	23	32	39	44
25	15	3	11	22	31	38
34	26	16	4	10	21	30
41	35	27	17	5	9	20
46	42	36	28	18	6	8
49	47	43	37	29	19	7

THE FATEFUL SQUARE OF SEVENS

ward Success, and the Spades the Difficulties and Troubles that face the enquirer.

Now read the cards in pairs, taking the right-hand and centre cards of the first row—remembering that in this method the left is the more powerful card of the two. Next read together the Master card and centre card of the top row. Bear in mind that each row is quite distinct and that no card is influenced by one above or below it, but only by the card on the left. You should particularly look out for all special cards, such as the type card indicating the enquirer; the Jack of his or her suit, representing the Thoughts; any special King, Queen, or Jack (representing young people) who may be in the enquirer's thoughts and in whom he or she may be interested. Then there is the Wish card (Nine of Hearts), the Disappointment card (Nine of Spades); the Tragic card (Ace of Spades); Money card (Ten of Diamonds); and Business card (Ten of Clubs).

Note the position of each of these cards and pay special attention to the significance of the cards that influence them. They all become of much greater importance and power if they are in the Master column—it is always unfortunate, however favourable the general run of the cards may be, if the Ace of Spades or Nine of Spades are Master cards. It is indeed wise after noting the suit importance of the whole mystical figure, to view, *in addition*, the suits of the Master cards by themselves. Should they be free from Spades, it would very greatly strengthen all the favourable influences in the general run of the cards.

This method of divination is a very fascinating one, and is, without any doubt, the most reliable for use for the diviner's own guidance.

It can be simplified for personal use by studying only

the suit values of the final mystic figure ; the suit values of
the Master cards themselves ; and the suit values of the
cards that influence (i.e. the cards on the left side of) the
special cards just named—the Type card, Wish card.
Disappointment card, and so on.

CHAPTER IX

THE TAROT OR DIVINATION CARDS

AFTER testing the various fascinating methods of "telling" the cards with an ordinary pack, most people will be anxious to test the powers of the ancient Tarocchi cards, as these were originally used solely for this purpose and not for gambling games.

We have already explained the peculiar arrangement of the pack, which contains seventy-eight cards, and we have suggested that a pack could easily be prepared at home. The pack is technically composed of two uneven sections—there were four suits, containing fourteen cards each, and this portion of the pack was known as the Minor or Lesser Arcana. In addition there were twenty-two other cards, all single, and without suits or sequence—these were known as the Major or Greater Arcana, and have never been used for any other purpose than divination.

The Major Arcana consists of twenty-one numbered cards and one unnumbered, and for practical purposes this series of simple numbers would be sufficient. If a pack can be purchased, the cards will probably be found numbered, in addition to having special designs upon them.

It is a curious fact that the Hebrew alphabet contains twenty-two letters, and it is claimed that there is a connection between the two. This may be the case, but the presence of an unnumbered card raises a difficulty—should

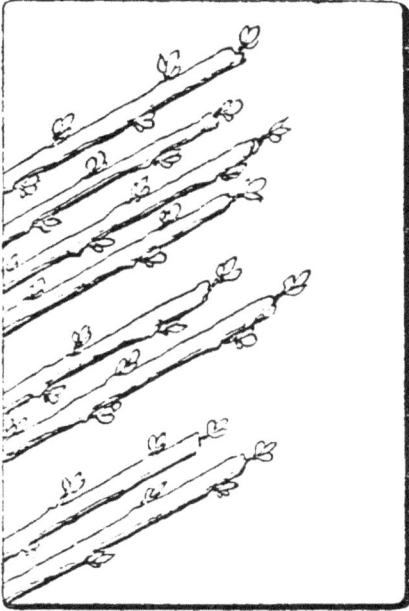

EIGHT of WANDS [CLUBS]

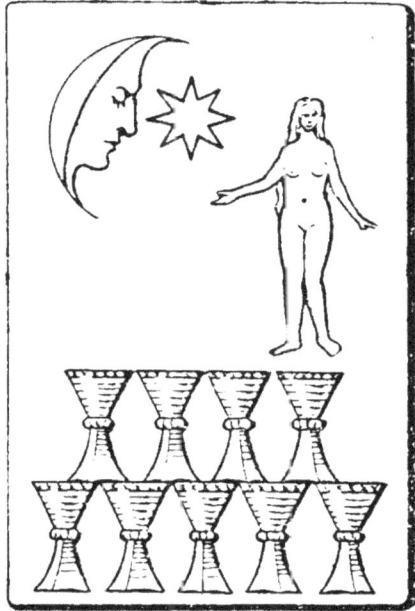

NINE of CUPS [HEARTS]

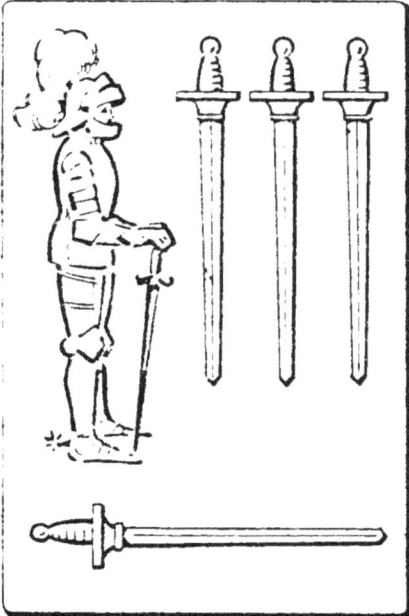

FOUR of SWORDS [SPADES]

ONE of PENTACLES [DIAMONDS]

TAROT OR DIVINATION CARDS

this come before number One, or after number Twenty-one.

It should also be noted that the twenty-one numbered cards fall naturally into three groups of seven cards each, and these have been claimed as representing the moral, mental and material groups, with the unnumbered card as the Deity. But the Tarocchi cards are extremely old, and had probably changed and evolved many, many times before we have any historical reference to them. It seems almost a certainty that there was no definite limit to the number of the earliest groups of articles used for divination, which would be actual articles collected by the seer, and not emblems as now used. Stones, seeds, bones—anything that could be preserved would serve the purpose of the earliest seers. With this we have little or nothing to do ; our purpose is to deal with the recognised set of card emblems forming the Tarot.

The first numbered card is known as the Magician or Juggler, and obviously the earliest meaning would be concerned with Magic, and not Jugglery, which is really a human amusement, whereas the Magician stood for all healing and creative powers, such as illness, pain, self-confidence, will-power, dexterity, and so on. It must be remembered with all these cards that a reversal of the card, top to bottom, also affects the meaning.

The second Tarot card is known as the High Priestess, and we know that in many early forms of worship women did act as priests—no doubt the men were otherwise employed searching for food and raiment for the family. Male priests were a much later development. This card represents secrets, mystery, science, knowledge, the unrevealed future.

For many purposes card number One is used to represent the enquirer if a man, while number Two is used if it is a woman. Again, in the case of a man, number Two would represent the woman in whom he is interested; and naturally in the case of a female enquirer number One card would represent the man about whom she is concerned.

The Third card represents Woman and the Fourth card Man—these are known as the Empress and Emperor, though it is obviously impossible for such titles to be the real original names, and personally we think it simpler to keep to Man and Woman.

The Woman represents fruitfulness, as would be natural. This covers action in its many forms. The Man, equally obviously, represents stability, power, protection, authority, and curiously enough the reversed card shows benevolence and compassion, thus suggesting brute force as one of the original meanings of this card.

The Fifth card is known as the Pope, and the original design has vanished in the course of the ages. It shows marriage, or servitude, and according to some writers, the man who will keep the woman enquirer. Reversed it does not carry any sinister meaning, but appears to represent casual society, the people we meet.

The Sixth card represents two Lovers, and obviously denotes affairs of the heart or of the home—in which case the reversed card indicates a broken love affair or other similar trouble after marriage.

The Seventh card is the Chariot, and stands for assistance, help, triumph over difficulties or over enemies. It may, in an unsatisfactory combination, show trouble, vengeance, and so on. The reverse shows defeat or quarrelling.

It is interesting to note that the cards are harmonious in the third degree—thus the First and Fourth cards are male, the Second and Fifth are priestly.

The Seventh is also sympathetic with the First and Fourth.

We will now deal with the second group of seven cards. Unfortunately numbers Eight and Eleven are often reversed; one early account gives Justice for number Eight and Courage for Eleven, another shifting them about. It is impossible nowadays to decide which is correct, though personally we prefer number Eleven for Justice.

Card number Eight then we will call Courage—it signifies energy or action, and generally is a successful and fortunate card. Reversed it does not necessarily mean ill-success, but abuse of power.

The Ninth card is known as the Hermit, and shows prudence and wisdom; but if the other cards are not good, it may merely mean trickery and lying. Reversed it shows secrecy, fear or needless caution.

Card number Ten represents the Wheel of Fortune, and it signifies Destiny. If this card turns up, the decision will concern some near event, and whichever way matters go, the result will be final and fateful. If reversed, this card shows an excessive result—abundance, superfluity, far more than is needful.

When considering the Eleventh card, we must recall what was said above—taking Courage for number Eight, we give Justice for number Eleven.

This does not mean Law, in our modern use of the word Justice, but the triumph of right. The diviner can only predict that right will succeed, and must leave it to the conscience of the enquirer to decide whether his own cause is indicated.

The Twelfth card is a most curious one and is known as the Hanged Man, but for some unknown reason he is represented as hanging by one foot, though not apparently in any way uncomfortable. It does not appear to be a form of punishment, for the card represents Wisdom, Intuition, Sacrifice—when reversed it stands for Selfishness and Greed. So we must assume that the so-called " Hanging " is intended to represent self-sacrifice.

The Thirteenth card is representative of Death, though its normal meaning merely indicates loss. Reversed, however, it is a most fateful sign. The card itself is generally ornamented with a full-length skeleton, much after the style of the well-known representation of Father Time.

The last card of this second series of seven is representative of Temperance, which of course is mental or physical, and has no connection with teetotalism. It means Carefulness, Economy, Good Management, and so on—reversed it is an important card, and shows divided interests.

It will again be seen that there is much sympathy in each couple of third cards—thus Eight and Eleven are often reversed ; while Nine and Twelve both indicate Prudence in affairs. Ten and Thirteen are obviously closely connected in the form of Destiny and Death, both representing Finality. The Fourteenth card, Temperance or Moderation, also follows the idea of the Eighth and Eleventh.

The third and final set of seven cards are really mystical, and to a great extent represent the force or influence of things beyond our own personal control. This group opens with number Fifteen as the Devil. The Malignant Power itself is generally represented in connection with a naked man and a naked woman, typical of Humanity, and intended to indicate our inability to get away from the unseen influences surrounding us. This card shows some powerful influence working in our lives in spite of ourselves, or in some cases our own physical inability to help ourselves owing to serious illness—in other words, as shown on the card, our naked or natural impotence. It need not necessarily be an evil influence, but it is one that we cannot resist. The old superstition, of course, was that every one of us had a good spirit behind our right shoulder, and an evil one behind our left. This superstition remains strong to-day. In its normal position this fateful card can be either good or evil, but reversed, it is invariably a bad sign.

The Sixteenth card also shows the strong force of the occult powers controlling our destinies, and it is invariably represented by a building struck and shattered by lightning. Its significance is Misery, Adversity, Disgrace, or even Ruin. It covers some unforeseen or unexpected calamity, as indicated by the lightning. When reversed, this card loses much of its malignity, though with bad cards near it might show imprisonment.

Following this shock, we have the Star for our next card, and as in so many other cases, a naked woman is shown. This card, number Seventeen, represents Hope, and when reversed the reading is unfortunate—Loss, Theft, or Privation of some sort.

The Eighteenth card shows us the Full Moon, looking down on an uncared-for path that apparently leads nowhere. It represents *Hidden* Dangers, Deception, Error of Judgment, and so on. Reversed it makes the deception our own—the enquirer will come to trouble or difficulty through his or her own deceit or falsehood. It is not a nice card for the unfortunate diviner, and care should be taken in the manner of our interpretation—in such cases it is better to suggest, and not to make any definite assertion.

The Nineteenth card is the Sun, with which is associated a naked child—generally a boy, as girls were not of much account in the East. The card is typical of Married Happiness, or at any rate of Domestic or Material contentment, according to the fall of the cards. When reversed, the power is merely lessened, not altered.

The Twentieth card is also a fateful one and is somewhat after the character of the Fifteenth, though not a sympathetic third card. But the reader will easily see that this idea does not apply to the final seven cards, all of which are mystic and individual in character. The card shows what is called the " Last Judgment," and is represented by the usual Western idea of an Angel, while below we see the graves opening and the dead rising. This card represents change of position, or if reversed, a loss of position. It will be noted that the change of position shown by the normal card can be for better or for worse ; here is the resemblance to the Fifteenth card.

The Twenty-first card, the last of the third series, is known as the Universe ; but it does not refer to this particular world of our own, which is often carelessly called the universe, but the *entire* Universe, Creation, everything that is or can be. It signifies great and continuing success, or if reversed an inability to raise oneself above one's present surroundings.

Apart from these three sets of seven cards there is always an extra unnumbered card, known to-day as the Fool— it is not exactly like the Jester of an ordinary pack of cards, but represents the " Extreme " in anything and everything, but not in a good sense. It is somewhat typical of modern life, all excitement and exaggeration. When reversed it represents the total neglect of our duties, negligence, carelessness, vanity—in fact, to use a modern word, " Swank " in its worst form.

The Minor Arcana, consisting of the four suits of fourteen cards each, does not represent quite the same series of ideas as are allotted to the modern pack. As it would be useless labour to commit to memory another set of meanings, we suggest that these could be written on the cards for guidance when " telling " the cards. The meanings are given in the following table:

Cups or Hearts.

King.—This can represent a fair man as with the ordinary pack of cards, but as a rule it shows kindness or warmth of heart. Reversed, suspicion, distrust.

Queen.—A fair woman, also success or happiness. Reversed it indicates interference by some woman.

Knight.—This Court card does not, of course, appear in the modern pack. It represents trust or confidence. Reversed, cunning or trickery.

Jack.—The Jack would represent a young person, either youth or maiden, if used for an individual. Otherwise it shows honesty of purpose, straightforwardness. Reversed, deception. In fact the meaning is very similar to that of the Knight.

Ten.—The Town where the enquirer lives ; in some cases the actual house itself. Apart from this, it shows the enquirer's position or local reputation. Reversed, it would indicate opposition and disputes, but of a local character, possibly in one's own household.

Nine.—Success or advantage. This is always a fortunate card, and the reversed position shows mistakes made by the enquirer, thus jeopardising success, but it does not indicate failure.

Eight.—This card represents friendship and affection. Reversed, the meaning is still good, but it shows gaiety or pleasure instead of affection. The good meaning becomes physical or material, instead of mental, or what we call of the *heart*.

Seven.—Some project the enquirer has in view. This meaning remains the same when the card is reversed.

Six.—In the normal position this card indicates that the " telling " refers to the past. If reversed it indicates the future, but it is the immediate future.

Five.—Marriage or some important ceremony. Reversed it indicates an arrival, some news, or a surprise.

Four.—Discontentment or displeasure. Reversed, a new acquaintance.

Three.—Success, a favourable ending to the enquirer's plan or wish. Reversed, the card indicates a quick result, not necessarily successful, but soon in point of time only.

Two.—Love, affection. Reversed, the card shows opposition to one's affection or by the person loved.

One.—Company, a pleasant gathering—the sort of thing we know as a " party." Reversed, we have a change of some sort, not necessarily good or bad, but a change.

It will be seen that the Heart suit is almost entirely fortunate in its normal position, while the reversed positions, on the whole, indicate delay rather than lack of success. An early design for this suit was the Acorn, which obviously represented successful agriculture, an essential feature of primitive life. Then came the Cup, also in its more modern fashion a sign of material success—or at any rate the necessary social position to enable you to entertain. The Western Heart is merely a careless adaptation of the old design of a Cup, just as the Cup itself was a careless or mistaken copy of the Acorn, possibly done in some country where the Oak tree was not prominent.

Wands or Clubs.

King.—A dark man, where an individual is indicated. Otherwise success. Reversed, danger that is threatening.

K

Queen.—A dark woman, or alternatively generosity. Reversed, the card shows a suspicious woman, mistrust, or evil threatening.

Knight.—A kind friend. Also carefulness, economy. Reversed, it suggests trouble through the carelessness of some such friend ; not intentional harm, but risk all the same.

Jack.—Order, management. Reversed, waste or even recklessness.

Ten.—The house or dwelling ; often the family of the enquirer if he or she is married. Reversed, loss or speculation involving risk.

Nine.—Honesty or discretion. Reversed, deceit or treachery.

Eight.—A dark girl. Beauty or innocence. Reversed, trickery by a woman.

Seven.—Money matters in general, business or inheritance. Reversed, the card indicates anxiety or worry over money matters.

Six.—Presents. Reversed, the card represents a longing for what we cannot get.

Five.—Love or affection. Reversed, the card calls for great discretion on the part of the diviner, as it may mean unfortunate but honest love, though it often means illicit or immoral passion, as in the case of a married woman.

Four.—Pleasure or enjoyment, of a somewhat material nature. Reversed, obstacles.

Three.—Dignity or position. Reversed, it often represents the children of the enquirer, or the beginning of some enterprise intended to improve the position of the enquirer.

Two.—Worry or difficulties. Reversed, it signifies a letter or message ; good, bad or indifferent.

One.—Contentment.   Reversed, money or assistance of some sort.

It will be seen that the Clubs form a good series in the normal way, but that the reversed positions are not generally so good as in the case of the Hearts.   Great care must be taken in noting the reversed cards, and it is wise to satisfy yourself as to the proportion of normal and reversed cards in all suits but the Hearts.   If there are more reversed cards than normal, you must allow for the serious cumulative effect of this reversal, and should study these reversed cards by themselves when giving your reading.

Diamonds also are a fairly fortunate suit, not unlike the Clubs in their general significance but more material, whereas Clubs are mental—thus there are two medium suits, with one fortunate and one unfortunate suit.   Diamonds are represented by money, either circular or roughly squared in shape—hence the modern diamond design—or much earlier by Pentacles, which may be described as a five-angled geometrical figure enclosed in a circle—hence the circular piece of money.

Pentacles or Diamonds.

King.—A man living in the country.   It should be noted that in the Tarot cards the Heart King represents all fair people, whereas in the modern pack we use both the red Kings, the Diamond type being darker than the Heart, which is almost blonde.   Otherwise, knowledge.   Reversed, the card shows advice, which may be good or bad in its result.   Alternatively a man who is dealing strictly though not necessarily unkindly with the enquirer.

Queen.—A woman living in the country.   Otherwise the love of money, or a craving for some monetary success.   Reversed, the card shows opposition or difficulty experienced in money matters.

Knight.—Departure, removal or separation from some one. If reversed, this will follow a quarrel. The separation or departure may, of course, prove to the enquirer's advantage, even if the card is reversed.

Jack.—A friendly stranger, or good news. Reversed, bad news or worry.

Ten.—Confidence or honesty of purpose. Reversed, treachery or deceit.

Nine.—Intelligence, observation, good management. Reversed, the card indicates obstacles or difficulties, certainly delay, but not necessarily with any bad result.

Eight.—Peace or order. Reversed, quarrels.

Seven.—Success, or some measure of advantage and profit. If reversed, the card shows hesitation and anxiety, but not necessarily any loss.

Six.—The hope, desire or wish of the enquirer, whatever it may be, whether material or of the affections. Reversed, it shows treachery, or unfaithfulness, if it concerns the affections.

Five.—Money, gain or inheritance. Reversed, it shows troubles or difficulties connected with money, such as legal cases, but not necessarily a loss of money, though almost certainly it shows that there will be no gain.

Four.—Company, society, pleasure. Reversed, this card is supposed to retain its normal meaning, which seems illogical and unlikely. We suggest that the reversal would indicate that the love of company was causing the enquirer to neglect more important matters.

Three.—Some business enterprise or undertaking. Reversed, the card represents the wish or attempt for some such enterprise or outlet where the fulfilment seems unlikely.

Two.—Money. Reversed, it signifies a surprise or some unexpected or unusual occurrence.

One.—The commencement of something. Reversed, it shows cruelty or misfortune.

On the whole, Diamonds is a fairly fortunate suit, but is far more mixed and vague in its influence than is the case with Hearts. Personally we prefer the Club suit, which suggests a rising above difficulties that lie in the enquirer's path, whereas Diamonds can better be described as a failure to use our powers or advantages to the utmost. The ultimate result may be, and often is, much the same, yet the effort indicated by Clubs speaks more for the character of the subject—such a person is more likely to succeed in the end. The fourth suit, Spades, is the unfortunate one.

Swords or Spades.

King.—Someone in authority or with power to affect the enquirer. Reversed, this will bring trouble and worry.

Queen.—Loss, absence or separation. Reversed, the card shows either a bad woman or one with a bad influence on the enquirer's life, or alternatively an unpleasant combination of partial success, though accompanied by worry

Knight.—Capability. Reversed, foolishness or conceit.

Jack.—Treachery. If reversed, the trouble will come from an unexpected source.

Ten.—Sorrow and tears. If reversed, it shows a passing success, lost almost as soon as realised.

Nine.—Good faith. If reversed, suspicion and doubt.

Eight.—Illness or blame. When reversed, the card shows an accident or some startling event.

Seven.—This card is not affected by being reversed, and shows hope and confidence, good advice.

Six.—Travel, a voyage, or a messenger—someone who has travelled. Reversed, it shows a surprise.

Five.—This card also is not affected by reversal, and means trouble, losses, sadness, mourning.

Four.—Solitude. Reversed, it indicates that the solitude is enforced, in some cases necessary economy after a loss.

Three.—Separation or a quarrel. If reversed, the enquirer will be responsible for the trouble.

Two.—Friendship. If reversed, it shows lying and deceit.

One—Prosperity. When reversed, this card generally shows an unfortunate love affair.

We will now give a few methods of reading from the full Tarot pack, but as it is an old system of divination, there are only a limited number of these, unlike those used with the modern pack, where we find at least a score of well-known systems of telling. In the first place, the enquirer must be quite certain as to time ; this must be made clear before the cards are touched. He or she must also decide whether a simple answer to a question is what he wants, or whether he prefers a general divination of the course of events. These points will control the seer's interpretation. It must also be remembered that with the Tarot cards the Ace is merely the One, and that the four Court cards are far more powerful than the commoner cards, and that the five higher commoner cards are correspondingly more powerful than the five lower ones, although the latter include the Ace.

A simple question can be answered by the general character of the cards, after they have been exposed by one or other of the recognised methods. You would count the various suits, and note the values of the cards in each. Indeed, it is a good plan to do this privately before beginning a general reading of the future, as it gives you a firm foundation upon which to build—many vague points can then be more clearly read, because you know roughly whether the immediate future is to be smooth or unfortunate.

The simplest method of arranging the Tarot cards is the one handed down by Monsieur Etteila. The full pack of seventy-eight cards must be shuffled by the enquirer, who then counts off three packs of twenty-six cards each. The seer picks up the centre pack and places it on the right.

Then the enquirer repeats the operation, but as there are now only fifty-two cards, he counts off three packs of seventeen cards each. This leaves an odd card, which is shuffled with the pack later on. The seer again removes the centre heap, but does not add to it the first heap reserved, but places them side by side.

For a third time the enquirer shuffles the pack, including the odd card, of course, and then counts off three packs of eleven cards each as before. There will be two odd cards, which are returned to the main pack after the seer has removed the centre heap of the third set of three.

Now the seer takes up the first heap removed and places each card, face upwards, in a straight line, going from right to left. There are, of course, twenty-six cards. In the same way the second heap is arranged below the displayed line, and as there are, of course, only seventeen cards, you begin somewhat more to the left. The final heap is similarly displayed below the second, and again it forms a shorter line.

The reading is given by the general run of suits and values in each line, and also by the special meaning of the individual cards. The bottom row will control the material or physical affairs of the enquirer ; the middle row governs his mental life, his friendships and affections, his hopes and so on ; while the top row represents the unseen influences at work on his or her life.

Another method on somewhat similar lines is as follows : The enquirer draws out one card to represent himself, and this is placed face upwards on the table. Then he must thoroughly shuffle the pack. Now the seer goes through the pack and builds up the rows of seven cards, working from right to left ; the first row being on top as in the previous method. But the cards must *not* be dealt in sequence—the first card placed on the table must be the top card of the pack after it has been shuffled ; the second card will be the *seventh* card from it in the pack, in other words, the original eighth card. This is placed to the left of the top card and forms the second card in the top row of seven. Then count out the next seventh card and place this as the third of the row, to the left of the second card. Obviously this will be the fifteenth original card in the shuffled pack.

Go on in this way, taking out every seventh card you come to, and adding it to the figure—the second row commencing as soon as you have displayed seven cards. To avoid confusion, it is wise to place each card not required at the bottom of the pack—thus you place the top card on the table, the second at the bottom of the pack, and count One ; the third below and count Two, and so on. You will find that the original bottom card will form the fifth card of the centre row on the table. The reading is given as in the first method.

A third method of telling the Tarot cards is known as the Great Figure of Fate. As it is rather complicated till you have actually tested it, we give a diagram to show how the cards should be used in order to build up the figure properly.

The enquirer must choose a card to represent himself, and this is placed in the centre of the table. The pack is now shuffled and handed to the seer, who deals the cards in proper sequence according to the numbers in the following diagram, the top card going at 1, the next card at 2, and so on. You will easily see that the figure forms a triangle

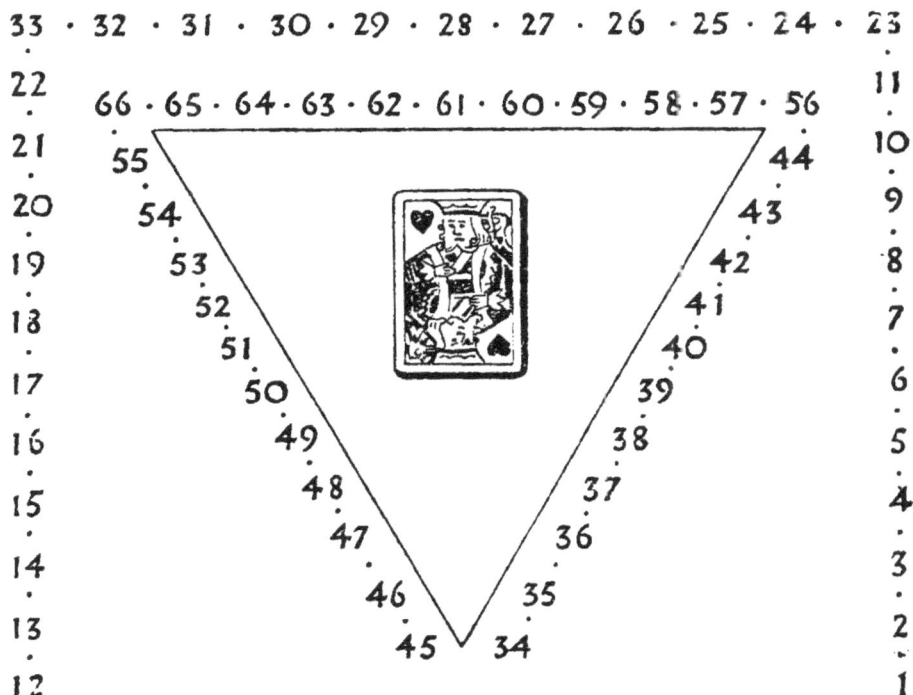

33 · 32 · 31 · 30 · 29 · 28 · 27 · 26 · 25 · 24 · 23

22
66 · 65 · 64 · 63 · 62 · 61 · 60 · 59 · 58 · 57 · 56   11
21   55   44   10
20   54   43   9
19   53   42   8
18   52   41   7
17   51   40
          50   39   6
16   49   38   5
15   48   37   4
14   47   36   3
            46   35
13   45 ∨ 34   2
12   1

THE GREAT FIGURE OF FATE

within a three-sided square. It is sometimes arranged in circles and in various fantastic forms, but the method we give is the simplest. In every case, whatever the design used, the reading is the same, so there is no advantage in using a complicated figure, unless you are anxious to mystify the enquirer.

The method of divination is based upon the idea that the right-hand eleven cards of the square and also of the triangle represent the Past; the uppermost row of square and triangle show the Present; while the left-hand eleven cards of each figure will indicate the Future.

The divination is made by combinations of three cards, of which the chosen card—representing the enquirer, and shown in the centre of the Triangle in the diagram—is always one. This card is combined with numbers 1 and 34, the two bottom cards of the series showing the Past; then with 2 and 35, and so on with each couple, for Past, Present, and Future.

Another simple method is for the enquirer to shuffle the pack, and then the seer arranges a row of seventeen cards in sequence, beginning with the top card of the pack. This makes the ninth card the exact centre, either from the right or from the left. The cards are read in threes, as in the Great Figure, but in this case the centre card represents the enquirer, and you pair from the ends. Thus you read cards 1, 9, 17 together for the immediate Present, or for some incident in the Past which the enquirer can name as a starting point—such as a recent business arrangement, a proposal of marriage, and so on. Then you read cards 2, 9, 16 together for a few days further ahead; numbers 3, 9, 15 for later still, and so on for the whole row. This method does not take long, and is considered very effective for dealing when a simple straightforward divination is required, such as in the cases indicated.

In conclusion, we would draw special attention to the question of reversed cards, which is of great importance in Tarocchi divination. After you have read the cards once it is obvious that the reversed cards would remain reversed, though they might not be dealt upon the table. To prevent this some tellers carefully arrange the pack with every card correctly upright before handing it to the enquirer. After the pack has been shuffled the enquirer must be asked to pull out a number of cards and reverse them without drawing them completely from the pack. This can be done in small blocks of a few cards each, or in two or three larger blocks, or by single cards, just as the enquirer prefers. But he or she must reverse at least one-third of the pack. When this has been done the pack is again shuffled before the laying out of the cards is commenced.

The Mayflower Press, Plymouth. William Brendon & Son, Ltd.

9 781608 641826